Money Management

for Those Who Don't Have Any

JAMES L. PARIS

HARVEST HOUSE PUBLISHERS

EUGENE, OREGON

Cover by Left Coast Design, Portland, Oregon

Cover photo © Julie Toy/Image Bank/Getty Images

MONEY MANAGEMENT FOR THOSE WHO DON'T HAVE ANY

Copyright ©1997 by Harvest House Publishers
Eugene, Oregon 97402
www.harvesthousepublishers.com

Library of Congress Cataloging-in-Publication Data

Paris, James L., 1965-
  Money management for those who don't have any / James L. Paris.—Updated ed.
    p. cm.
Includes bibliographical references (p.).
  ISBN 0-7369-1337-8 (pbk.)
  1. Finance, Personal. I. Title.
  HG179.P2294 2004
  332.024—dc22   2003022572

Printed in the United States of America

04 05 06 07 08 09 10 11 / VP-KB / 10 9 8 7 6 5 4 3 2 1

To Robert G. Yetman, Jr.,

*my researcher who behind the scenes makes
every one of my books a reality and rarely
gets any public recognition for his important
contribution to each and every word "I" write.*

Contents

Taking the
Winning Approach

I hope you enjoy reading this book as much as I have enjoyed writing it. Even us financial writers enjoy the fun of a project like this which makes interpreting charts and graphs and explaining the economy pale by comparison. I have always felt that there is too little financial and consumer information for the hard-working, middle-class family. The media, as intent as they are to focus on "how tough things are," continually fail to provide an answer for the typical American family's financial woes. Most news broadcasts offer brief information regarding how the stock market may have done that day—if they provide you with anything financial at all. The truth is that for most, making it to the next paycheck is of far greater concern than how the stock market is performing. I know, because I grew up in a blue-collar family and am well aware of the phrase "we can't do that because we don't have any money."

My parents never once discussed the Dow Jones Industrial Average around the dinner table.

You may have experienced this book jumping off the shelf and into your hands after you read the title. But are you really without money? Could it be that your problem is more about ending up without any money than not having it in the first place? Many people become insolvent through a process of bad decisions—not an inability to earn money.

In my seminars, I often use the analogy of a bucket. If you have a bucket with a hole in it, yet continue to pour water in it— what will the end result be? That's right—an empty bucket. So in response to money problems, what if we decide to increase the amount of water we are pouring in the bucket? I imagine you are starting to see my point. This is not a "water problem." It is a "bucket" problem! Such is the struggle of many middle-class American families. Their financial management is tantamount to the leaky bucket. No matter how much money they earn, they always end up with nothing.

This book focuses on two elements of money-management challenges. First, it includes hundreds of ways for you to get along with little or no money. Second, you'll find hundreds of strategies to help you plug that leaky bucket—or at least decrease the leak to a slow drip.

If you are a reader of my previous books, you know that I believe that our money-management approach as Christians is far more significant than simple economics. Once you truly understand that you must surrender your finances to the Lord (like every other part of your life), you can begin to see the bigger picture.

Our greatest responsibility is not how much we accomplish for ourselves, but what we can do with our finances that will bring glory to God.

There is an inherent special challenge in life for those who have little, if any, financial resources. Interestingly enough, the parable of the talents (Matthew 25:14-30) gives us a perspective on what this challenge truly is. Jesus shares a story about a master who goes on a long journey. Before he left, he entrusted his property to his three servants. To one, he gave five units of money; to another, two units; and to the last, one unit. Then he left on his journey. Upon his return, he asked each servant for an accounting of what he had done with his property. While the first two had each doubled the money they were entrusted with, the third servant had no increase. In fact, the principal excuse given for the lack of any increase from this servant was, "I was afraid."

I find it fascinating that the one who had the least did the least. Maybe there is an inherent fear in having nominal financial resources. Perhaps the disadvantage is more perceived than real. In any case, many who are struggling financially continue to struggle because of wrongly focusing their energies. Most think about what they don't have and how difficult things are instead of finding what they can do to solve the problem.

Money problems are often not solved directly by money but through creativity. When Ross Perot ran for president in 1992, he was criticized by some of his former employees about his frugal spending approach to his businesses. He made his frugality clear when he got a $10 dollar haircut at the same time that Bill Clinton received his infamous $200 haircut on the runway at Los Angeles International Airport. A significant part of keeping money once you get it has to do with your ability to be frugal.

Frugality is really having the discipline to spend less than you really can. Ross Perot can certainly get any kind of haircut he wants, but he chooses to get the ten dollar one. (Some would point out that he is getting what he pays for!) Although no one wants to be called cheap or frugal, it is without question a key element to achieving your financial goals, regardless of where you are at right now.

Money Management for Those Who Don't Have Any is a winning approach even for those who have money. Consider the fact that two automobiles going the same speed and having the same destination will each consume a different amount of fuel. Being a coupon-savvy, penny-pinching, discount-hunting fanatic will increase your financial mileage. Being frugal with your finances simply means that you choose not to be a "money guzzler." You make the strategic decision to spend less—not to enjoy life less. You can get to the same destination for less money and enjoy the process just as much.

To those without money and those with it, I wish you success in your pursuit of good stewardship.

> *Rich and poor have this in common:*
> *The LORD is the Maker of them all.*
> — PROVERBS 22:2

Financial Freedom
on a Budget

Budgeting. It strikes fear in the hearts of many Americans throughout every nook and cranny of this great nation. Many of us are able to get by without the implementation of and adherence to a formal budget, but if you're feeling as though money is very tight at any given time of the month, chances are you're not one of them.

A lot of people resist designing a budget because they perceive the need to do so as a sign of weakness—that having to put such things to paper is an indication that they're not able to handle their money in a more mature fashion. There are two reasonable responses to such a notion: "Hogwash!" and "You're absolutely right!"

First, all businesses must keep track of what they take in and what they spend each month. Why should you look at your family as being any different than that of a business? Personal interactions aside, a family's financial profile is just the same as a business's financial profile in that families, like businesses, take in money each month and have bills which must be paid. If a business feels it is prudent to keep a written account of revenue inflow and outflow, why shouldn't you?

There is, however, the other response which is perfectly reasonable: Maybe you can't properly manage your money without the aid of a written budget. You don't need to feel bad or self-conscious about this. Some people need a little bit of extra help to keep proper track of their money. Self-discipline is not always present in vast quantities within many people, and it takes time to be developed. In the process, you should give yourself some assistance. A formal, written budget is the best way I can think of.

Before you jump right in and put a budget together, you must first take steps to ensure that you have maximized your inflow and minimized your outflow as much as possible. In other words, the formal budget should be set up only *after* you have made a number of significant lifestyle changes which are conducive to prudent financial living. To that end, here are a number of tips and strategies (some philosophical in nature, others more practical) which should be reviewed and applied before the budget is implemented.

TAKING ACTION
Conquer the "I DESERVE what I can afford" myth.

If you conducted a poll on why so few of us are able to jump off the paycheck-to-paycheck treadmill permanently, you would likely find that the reasons all center around the accumulation of bills, which most perceive to be necessary. Not the bills—the *accumulation* of the bills. Many people who work hard believe that they are entitled to rack up a string of bills (most typically on their credit cards) so that they may enjoy fruits which their same labors would have paid for outright years ago.

How many times have you heard someone mutter in passing conversation as he reached into his wallet and pulled out his plastic money, "I work hard. I deserve to do something nice for myself now and again." A large and growing number of the populace is perpetually tempted by the plethora of material goods splashed across our TV sets each night. (Now there's a good reason to keep the thing turned off!) Many people have talked themselves into believing that they deserve those things—regardless of income level. This is just not true. They are doing themselves and their families a disservice by believing that it is.

I believe that the "I deserve it" excuse is the prevailing reason for much of America's financial woes. This also appears to be a prominent source of disagreement in marriages. The restriction of spending by one partner is perceived by the other as depriving him or her of a "need" or "something deserved."

We all dislike having to go without. What's more, we especially dislike asking those dependent upon us to go without since we feel responsible for their circumstances (and rightly so). The fact remains, however, that one of the quickest routes to financial insolvency lies in believing that we have the right to purchase what we cannot afford. As a steward of God's money, you *don't* have that right. No one is going to stop you from making a purchase which is not in your best interest financially, and to that extent you *do* have the right to engage in such imprudency. When you look at such purchases in the proper perspective, however, your "right" disappears.

From this moment forward, resolve to view the justification for the purchases you make on the basis of affordability and God's direction rather than on the basis of your perception of deservability. This is a solid, key step to bringing your spending under control and ultimately ensuring that more money remains in your pocket at the end of each month. Keep in mind that we are only attempting to resolve the matter of negative cash flow, that is, spending more than you have to spend. We have not yet crossed the threshold of actually creating a surplus that can be saved for future needs such as retirement and your children's college educations.

TAKING ACTION
You don't have to have some of everything.

This principle is somewhat of a continuation of the previous one. It's foolish to buy into the notion that because everyone else has something, you must have it as well. A lot of people spread their financial resources very thin in an effort to make sure they have at least one of everything: cable television, a new car, a new stereo, and so forth.

Who are you trying to impress? Hopefully, not the neighbors. After all, will the neighbors bail you out when your resources can no longer support your spending habits? Maybe you're really trying to impress yourself, your spouse, or your children.

Well, if you're trying to dazzle them with the accumulation of material possessions, you may have bigger problems than can be handled within the confines of this book. The truth is, refusing to become a slave to fashion and trends will assist you greatly in bringing your spending under control and making your budget much more manageable. Resolve from this point forward to reduce as much as possible (hopefully that means *completely*) unnecessary purchases. A simple exercise is to ask the question,

Why do I want this? And, of course, be honest enough with yourself to ponder a legitimate answer before proceeding.

Although we all have legitimate needs, using the justification of a "need" to purchase a satellite dish, a new boat, or any other extravagance is purely ridiculous.

TAKING ACTION

Resist impulse buying by adopting the "walk away" approach to making purchases.

One of the most effective methods of combating impulse buying I've ever come across is what I call the "walk away" approach. What in the world is that, you ask? Well, the next time you're in a mall and you see something you like and want to buy, just *walk away*. That's right. Turn your back on the item and move on or head for the door. What I tell people is that if they successfully resist making the purchase when they first see the item and go home, then they can determine if they liked what they saw so much that they would be willing to go back to the store to buy it. If you're one of the many Americans prone to impulse buying, you might be surprised to learn that a great many people, upon reflection, decide that they *don't* want the item they thought they wanted when it was staring them in the eye. If you come to the conclusion that you still want the item once you get home, at least you have given yourself and your budget the benefit of putting some thought into the purchase—and the purchase will not have been made on impulse.

Make no mistake about it, many a family's finances have been ruined by members giving in to impulsive buying urges. To make sure your family does not become one of those families, adopt the "walk away" response or some other quality measure of your own devising to avoid impulse buying.

By the way, I am not saying that you need to always walk away from any purchase you consider making. If you make a trip to the mall to buy some shirts because you truly need shirts, then by all means buy them. Going to the mall or store for a specific purpose demonstrates that you've already put some thought into your prospective shopping, removing it from the category of "impulse" and into the category of "necessary," or at least "thoughtful."

TAKING ACTION
Reduce your expenses as much as possible.

The first reaction of many people after reading this strategy might well be, "No kidding!" The sad fact is that many people have not resolved to keep all of their expenses as minimal as possible. Expense-reduction is really a state of mind. It is a constant effort on your part to find ways to save money in all facets of your life. When you go out to dinner, for example, do you really need to buy an appetizer along with your meal? When you buy a car, is it necessary to opt for power windows, or will you do just fine rolling them up yourself? Do you really need to purchase movie or other premium channels along with your basic cable package? The truth is, as good a job as we all think we're doing in reducing our outflow, most of us could do a lot better. My wife and I have participated for years in what we call family financial meetings. At these meetings we go over our written budget and make a game of coming up with ideas on how to save money. These meetings have been extremely valuable exercises. It is amazing to me that, even being a financial planner and author on finance, there is so much waste in my own spending. This waste is typically not discovered unless we take the time to sit down and make it a priority to look at all of our outflow of money and ask the question, Why?

TAKING ACTION
Set aside a portion of your income to develop a cash reserve.

One of the toughest things for a family budget to overcome is the occasional emergency or other necessary expense which will arise from time to time. If the engine falls out of your car, what then? Do you pay for the repairs by using your credit card or by borrowing money from the bank or some other entity? Many of us do, but that's the wrong solution. Increasing your debt load and paying substantial interest charges to boot only add to your budgetary difficulties. So will cleaning out your checking account to pay for the repairs. What, then, is the answer?

The answer is to set aside an emergency fund to cover unexpected expenses. A good rule of thumb is to save between three and six months' worth of living expenses. The more generous you can be to your cash reserve account, the better. I am usually asked at my seminars what is the best method of determining how much to put away. The answer is not a simple one. However, one way of thinking it through is to consider the various scenarios that have some possibility of happening in your circumstances. For example, if you're a college professor with tenure you are unlikely to face an unemployment crisis. On the other hand, if you are a construction worker you may face a period of unemployment every year. A number of other issues to consider include your insurance coverages, your health, and your past experience of needing to tap into emergency funds.

Once you have a substantial amount of money set aside, you have lowered your exposure to financial risk. By developing such a fund, you can even help soften the blow of unemployment—a circumstance which can easily drive an ill-prepared family into bankruptcy. In the past when I've mentioned the idea of setting aside a portion of income for this purpose, some people have suggested that doing so will only put further strain on a budget already on life-support. I might agree with that if you're in such dire straits that you are practically out in the street and need every single dime for day-to-day subsistence. But I don't agree with that notion otherwise. First of all, building a cash reserve will take a little time, so don't try to put away $400 or $500 each month. Start out with what you can afford—even if it's just $25 or $30 each month. As I've said, many people who are broke at the end of the month can almost always find areas where some money is being wasted. So, for most of us, it is quite possible to allocate money to a cash reserve fund without adding to your family's financial hardships. Furthermore, think of what may happen if you *don't* have such an emergency fund in place when disaster strikes.

What should you do with the money you've decided to set aside for a cash reserve? I think that using a mutual fund as a holding place is a good idea. There is more discussion on mutual funds in chapter 5.

TAKING ACTION

Increase your income
as much as possible.

I'm reminded of a conversation I had once with a young, single fellow who was having a hard time making ends meet. He was working 40 hours a week and living quite frugally, which included sharing an apartment with two other gentlemen. Upon examination, it was obvious that he didn't have a lot of room to decrease his expenses; he'd already cut those to the bone. Interestingly, however, it apparently had never dawned on him to get another job in addition to the one he already held. This person had bought into the notion that so many others have bought into—that in America all you should need is one job to "make it."

Unfortunately, that's not always true anymore. Many people are finding that they must work 50 to 60 hours each week in order to live as they would like. While I would be the first to admit that working more is probably not in the best interest of a quality home life, this philosophy must now be kept in the perspective of American living in the twenty-first century. (The principal reason that so many families must have two spouses working is our tax system. In the 1950s the average American family paid about 3 percent of their income in taxes, now it is nearly 30 percent.)

Before you turn your nose up at the thought of taking a second job for a few hours a week, sit down with a pencil and paper and figure out how much a few extra hours of work might help your finances. Furthermore, keep in mind that you'll be spending more time away from your family, but your extra income will undoubtedly provide the means to enjoy more diversions and entertainment when you're all together. Again, it's a balancing

act. Don't nix the extra job option without thoroughly research-
ing its potential for you and your family.

Another option which can help you earn extra income without requiring a great deal of time away from your family is to
start a small business. Many people have started successful small
businesses which they run out of their homes—and the tax deductions they've received by doing so have gone a long way to
limiting the tax bite.

Always remember that there are two parts to a family's financial profile: what they earn and what they spend. Too many
people choose to concentrate only on eliminating expenses when
they find themselves in the midst of a budgetary crunch. While
that can be your first move—and it's understandable that most
of us don't want to increase our work loads—it's possible (and,
in fact, very easy) to add substantially to your income. Consider
picking up a second job or starting a home-based business.

TAKING ACTION
Adopt a plan to divide any extra money between your debts and your savings.

Once you've paid your bills and other obligations each
month, you may find that you have some money left (maybe not
now, but once you implement the strategies outlined in this
chapter you will!). How should you deal with this extra cash?
Some people may be inclined to spend all of the leftover money
on themselves, believing that they deserve (there's that word
again) to do so in light of the fact that they've been so good
about sticking to their budgets and paying their bills. Others may

take a more prudent course, using the money to pay down credit card bills faster or perhaps allocating the funds toward savings and investment plans which build toward the future. Which do you think I'm going to recommend? . . . You might be surprised. . . .

Whenever you have money left over at the end of the month or come into some extra cash in the form of overtime earnings or any other windfall, do both you and your budget a favor. Split the money between the two of you. It's no secret that sticking to a budget may not be much fun. It can be very trying at times, particularly for those people for whom such self-discipline does not come easy. One of the best ways that you can help alleviate that stress is by committing to be good to yourself and your family's finances whenever you have a little extra cash. This doesn't mean you should take all the money and spend it on frivolity. It means you should implement a system by which you apportion a fixed percentage of such sums into your two primary avenues: spending and debt reduction.

If, for example, you come into an extra $500, you might want to take $250 for you and your family to spend and use the other $250 for debt reduction or savings and investment accounts. Remember that extra money doesn't have to be spent or allocated in an all-or-nothing fashion. Give yourself and your family a chance to have some fun—but not at the expense of your bills or your savings accounts. If you feel that you don't need as much as $250 for your own pleasure or recreational spending purposes, you can adjust the amount as you see fit . . . but you get the idea.

TAKING ACTION
Credit cards are not assets; they are liabilities.

I wonder if there is anyone reading this book who doesn't have at least one credit card in his or her pocket? Living on debt, and on credit card debt in particular, has become an all-too-common way of life for many Americans. This lifestyle has become so common that a lot of us are inclined to look at our credit cards as being part of our asset base. After all, we can use them to purchase goods, pull cash out of ATM machines, and even write checks against the accounts they represent. Furthermore, credit cards are called plastic money, so it's no different than if it were green paper with a picture of a dead president on it, right?

In all honesty, credit cards should be called a plastic *loan* because that's what they really do. They loan you money. If you are going to bring your budget under control, one of the first things you should do is look at the credit cards you carry in the proper perspective—as sources of cash outflow, not inflow. We've all seen the TV commercials displayed by one of the leading credit card companies that talk about how convenient it is to use their product to do such things as purchase gasoline and groceries. Well, yes, it's convenient—but it's also a big mistake. Whenever you consider a purchase and don't have the funds in the bank to cover it, do you factor in the amount of room you have left on your credit card(s) to decide if you can afford to make the purchase? Don't do it. Look at this another way. When you fill out a loan application, rental agreement, or other similar personal financial inventory, and you are asked about your credit card balances, is that information under the heading "Assets" or "Liabilities"? Get the picture?

Destroy all but
two or three credit cards.

Because credit card debt is a leading cause of destruction in household budgets, it becomes imperative to rid yourself of those things as quickly as possible. Go through your wallet(s) and pull out all of your credit cards, as well as your department store charge cards. You and your spouse should sit down together and decide which cards you will keep—and destroy the rest.

Why do you need more than two or three cards, anyway? Is there a good reason for it? Probably not. Sure, having six or seven bank credit cards and two store charge cards may give you a lot more "spending power," but what it *really* gives is a lot more "indebtedness power." Don't be fooled: True spending power comes in the form of real cash, from having money in the bank. Besides, all of the big-name department stores and gas stations I know of take Visa and MasterCard, so you aren't excluding yourself from any party by limiting yourself to carrying one of those credit cards.

At this point you might be thinking, "Hey, that's good advice. But why do I need to carry any credit cards at all?" Well, that's a good question. The truth is, if you're having that tough of a time controlling your credit card spending habits, you might *have* to relinquish all of your plastic in order to secure your budget. However, in all of this talk about the evils of credit cards, let's not lose sight of their chief advantage: They offer you a great deal of flexibility and safety when you're on vacation or have an emergency of some sort. Most rental car companies, for example, still won't welcome your business unless you have a credit card. And having a piece of plastic will lower your theft exposure on vacations. Furthermore, if you get stranded by the side of the road somewhere and need to pay for a tow truck or need to access some food or assistance when cash is not available, a credit card can be the answer to your problems. Therefore, it's probably not a good idea for you to simply trash all of your credit cards. Rather, pick one or two which are widely accepted and dump the rest. This way you secure the advantages of the credit card but also begin to lower the damage that the cards can do to your budget.

TAKING ACTION
Do not carry very much cash.

One of the best and simplest ways available to ensure you will limit your wasteful spending as much as possible is by limiting the amount of cash you carry when you're out and about. For most of us, it's difficult not to be tempted by the wad of cash in our pockets, even though we know better than to spend it. If I'm out and I see something I want, it's so simple to just reach in my pocket and pull out the money to pay for it. If I didn't *have* the money available, however, spending it would not be such an easy proposition. Oh, I'll always have at least a little with me, but never so much that I'll be able to buy anything substantial with it. Sure, I could still purchase the item in question without going further into debt if I have my checkbook or debit card with me, but psychologically speaking I find that it takes more effort to use those spending tools. For many of us, the look and feel of paper money can be quite intoxicating, and it can lead us to act in a fashion that is against our better interests. The best solution is to remove the temptation and keep as little cash as possible available to you.

Dedicate yourself to becoming a bargain shopper.

I know a lot of people, including myself, who have saved a lot of money over the years by making a concerted effort to do so. One of the best ways to save money is to remain on the lookout for great deals, coupons, rebates, and any other kind of money-saving offers which are presented on behalf of the goods and services you're interested in purchasing. However, in order for this to work and to help you save some serious money in the long run, you're going to have to really dedicate yourself to saving money—make it a lifestyle commitment.

Cash-Saving Coupons

Do you clip coupons? Why not? Are you self-conscious, as many people are, about appearing too thrifty in the eyes of the general public? Get over it! The fact is you can save yourself a boatload of money by using coupons. Do you belong to any of those wholesale shopping clubs? Again, why not? By purchasing many of your day-to-day goods, as well as some of your entertainment or less-frequently purchased household goods from these establishments, you can realize a huge savings both in the short run as well as in the long run. (My wife is a coupon hawk and has earned a reputation as such. While I was writing this chapter, she interrupted me [a welcome interruption, I might add] to say that she got our van detailed for only $7 by using a coupon, as opposed to the normal charge of $25.)

One of the best ideas I know of to save money quickly and easily is to start an organized file of coupons. Whenever you see coupons or certificates which offer discounts on any goods or services which you may have an occasion to purchase, cut them out and put them in your file. Take care to divide your file into several categories, from "Household Products," to "Food," to "Automotive Care," and every other category you can think of. Maintaining a ready file of coupons and other discount offers will prove to be one of your better tools in keeping your budget in a constant state of repair. I also let my coupons guide my spending. For example, if I am planning to go out to dinner with my wife I might go through the coupon book and choose from those that I have a coupon for. This doesn't usually limit my options in a big way. By doing this, I might have enough money to go out on two dates with her that week instead of just one. A great coupon book for this that is available in most major cities is "The Entertainment Coupon Book"(for more information call Entertainment Publications at 800-477-3234). General coupons are also available at my website: www.christianmoney.com.

Classified Ad Bargains

When you seek to purchase sporting equipment, large household goods, or other durable items, make it a habit to peruse the classified section of your local newspaper. Very often you will find items you want advertised for sale in the paper by people who must sell them quickly or who simply don't care how much they get for them. If you see something advertised for sale which says "$350 or best offer," feel free to make an offer which is lower than $350. The best way to know how much to offer is to make an appointment to go down and look at the item. This way, you will be able to make an offer which is perhaps lower than what is desired by the seller but not outright silly. If the seller chooses not to accept your offer, so what? Keep looking, making certain to offer bids which preserve your best interests as well as those of the seller. The newspaper can be an excellent source of quality used goods. If your paper covers a large enough area, you should never have a shortage of places to go or people to see.

Garage Sales

Garage sales are another excellent source of bargains. This is particularly true of those put on by people who are moving, because they will be more likely to get rid of quality items. The key to not getting tripped up at a garage sale, however, is to keep from purchasing things that you don't truly need. My mother, who is a garage-sale expert, exposed me to that concept at a very early age. I remember going "garage saling"(as she called it) on each and every Friday for years. Yes, I was dragged along in the car. I usually didn't mind it, since I was able to cash in on the opportunity by convincing Mom to buy a few things for me as well.

Your shopping habits should be no different for garage sales than they are for trips to the mall. Go and seek only what you've decided in advance you really need, making sure not to get caught up buying things you're not there to specifically buy.

In my experience, bargain shopping is not difficult, but it does take a certain amount of resolve. Most Americans have become accustomed to finding the easy way to get something done—even if it means spending a little more money. The problem is, spending a little more money in the short run usually adds up to having spent a *lot of money* in the long run.

TAKING ACTION

Always use a list
for grocery shopping.

Of all the usual money-spending habits you'll engage in over the course of your lifetime, food shopping can be among the costliest. It is nothing at all for a family of four to spend in excess of $150 on the weekly trip to the supermarket, and many spend much, much more. Combine that amount with the incidentals picked up during the rest of the week, and it is easy to see how a family of four can put well over $200 into the coffers of grocery merchants each week.

There are a lot of ways to limit the amount of money spent at the supermarket. I've already discussed the wisdom behind actively using coupons and purchasing memberships to bargain wholesale shopping clubs. There is, however, an even simpler way to ensure that your weekly trips to the supermarket don't cost you any more than they absolutely should: Before you go, make a list.

There are two aspects to using a weekly grocery list properly. The first is *using*. The very fact that you sit down to make a list in the first place will force you to put more thought into what you're buying, which allows you to refrain from purchasing what you *don't* need. The second aspect to grocery-list shopping involves using it as a tool for you and the rest of your family to decide what will be purchased that week.

The key is to instill in each family member the understanding that your food purchases each week are to be governed absolutely by the list. If it isn't on the list, it's not purchased. Once in the grocery store there is to be no weakening, no cheating, nothing. Once you deprive the list of the power to help control your food shopping behavior, its usefulness is nullified. I know of one family who is so dedicated to the grocery list, they let themselves go without in the event they forgot to write down a perfectly reasonable and necessary item. That may strike some people as being rather extreme behavior, but these particular folks have become so enamored of the help they've received by adhering so rigidly to the grocery list that they absolutely forbid themselves from straying from it even a little bit.

All of this talk about the importance of a grocery list may seem somewhat trivial, but it's not. We've shown how much money can be spent on groceries each week, and if implementing a grocery list mentality within each member of the family can allow you to save significant amounts of money each week, your budget will be much happier for it.

TAKING ACTION
Plan the family's meals on a weekly basis.

This principle is a continuation of the previous one. In order to construct a usable, money-saving shopping list, you will have to plan the family's meals in advance. Put a lot of thought into your evening meals since these have the potential to be your costliest. Decide in advance which, if any, meals will be eaten out. Again, incorporating this principle may subject you and your family to a level of regimentation and discipline which may be uncomfortable at first, but don't lose sight of what prompted you to buy this book in the first place. Be sure to buy *all* of the food you'll need for your meals in advance. (This leaves you with no reason to make another money-spending visit to the grocery store.)

TAKING ACTION
Limit the number of meals you eat outside the home.

American families spend a lot of money eating out each week. Yours may be one of them. If you're not convinced as to how costly that endeavor can be, save your restaurant receipts for one week and total them up. In this day and age, even a trip to McDonald's for a family of four had better not be made unless you've got a 20-dollar bill in hand. While I recommend that you *do* avail yourself of the opportunity to eat out once in a while if possible (for sanity's sake), keep the excursions to restaurants down to a minimum. When your newfound financial prudence leads you to financial independence one day, you can then eat out every night of the week if you wish. Until then, however, watch your budget carefully.

Another frequent money-waster which many working people indulge in each and every workday is the ritual of going out to eat lunch. For the cost of a modest lunch, you can purchase enough deli meats and other lunch foods in the supermarket to feed yourself for an entire week. If you're resistant to this idea because you're afraid of how "brown bagging" your lunch each day will look to your coworkers, don't be. If this book is in your hands, it's because either your finances are in sad shape or you at least perceive that they are. Whichever it is, what coworkers think should be the least of your concerns. Your family's welfare is all that should matter at this point.

TAKING ACTION

Implement a system to pay off your bills.

Other than limiting the size of your monthly consumption bills (such as utilities and groceries), you must deal with the horde of bills you have which account for the various loans (I'm including credit card purchases and lines of credit here) you have taken out to purchase cars, boats, clothes, or whatever. It is these bills and the accompanying interest charges that help keep them high which can really take an unspeakable toll on a family's finances. Half of your battle is to limit greatly, if not eliminate altogether, your use of these loans and lines of credit to purchase goods and services. Once that is done, however, you are still left to deal with the balances which remain from the past purchases. To help preserve your family's financial stability as well as your own sanity, you would do well to develop a system to begin to pay off your loans and credit bills in full.

There are a couple of different schools of thought regarding how to systematically pay down these bills. Both systems are perfectly legitimate and helpful. The first method involves paying the bills down in order from lowest balance to highest balance. The thinking behind utilizing a "lowest balance" method is that it allows you to relatively quickly pay off a few bills entirely, giving you a distinct psychological advantage as you engage in your bill-paying efforts. You will want to make the minimum payments on each one of your other bills while you allocate the rest of your bill-paying monies toward paying off the bill at hand. Once the bill at hand has disappeared, move on to the next.

The other system you can use to pay off your bills involves paying them off in the order from highest interest rate to lowest. The benefit of this payment method is that it allows you to make a quicker dent in your total indebtedness because you focus on the costliest bills first.

Both of these bill payment systems are reasonable and quite effective. Again, the key to using them successfully is to make the minimum payment on each of your bills except on the one you're in the process of ridding yourself of permanently. If your budget allows you to make a little more than the minimum on the others, so be it—that way, you won't have as far to go when it comes time to focusing on those.

Creating and Implementing the Budget

Up to now, we have discussed very broad philosophies as well as tangible money-management mechanisms which are designed to help you bring your spending and budgetary concerns under better control. In order to get to a point where you can live in accordance with a budget, these rudimentary steps must be taken first. Now that you have completed the first level of family financial management, you are ready to move on to the second level: the creation and implementation of the actual budget itself.

TAKING ACTION

Write down goals you wish to meet
with family revenue.

In order to ensure that the budget you create is as comprehensive and as helpful as possible, one of the first steps is to gather the family and have a discussion as to what short-term and long-term goals you would all like to see met by way of the budget. I'm not talking about the meeting of your usual month-to-month obligations; it's a given that you want to be sure to meet those with your budget. What I'm talking about is the creation of a list which includes such things as a new car, a vacation, the kids' college education, a new house, retirement, and so on. These goals may be ones which you have planned to meet over a variety of time periods: a vacation next year, a new house in ten years. Either way, you will want to include these goals in your budget so you will have completely accounted for everything you wish to fund. Too many people make the mistake of including just the day-to-day and month-to-month expenses of running a household when creating their budgets, neglecting to include the other items which they would also like to see happen.

It is very important when developing a list of these goals, to concentrate on ascribing an estimated cost to each one of them. You must be able to get some idea about how much money you'll need to set aside each month to meet these goals.

By the way, if you're in a situation where you're flat broke at the end of each month, all of this talk about funding vacations and new cars may seem somewhat distasteful. However, do not be discouraged. Once you have begun implementing the other principles contained in this book, you will soon have the ability to allocate your monthly revenue toward short- and long-term goals like those outlined here. I fully understand that this is not something you may be able to do right off the bat, but I have no doubt that you'll be able to do it soon enough.

Cash Flow Chart

Monthly Income

Salary . . . .   _____

Commissions . . . .   _____

Gratuities . . . .   _____

Alimony . . . .   _____

Child support . . . .   _____

Unemployment or worker's compensation . . . .   _____

Other income . . . .   _____

Other income . . . .   _____

Total Income   _____

Monthly Expenses

Mortgage/Rent . . . .   _____

Groceries . . . .   _____

Electricity . . . .   _____

Water . . . .   _____

Telephone . . . .   _____

Other utilities . . . .   _____

Car payments . . . .   _____

Car expenses . . . .   _____

Insurance (life/health) . . . .   _____

Homeowners/renters insurance . . . .   _____

Car insurance . . . .   _____

Credit card payments . . . .   _____

Other loan payments . . . .   _____

Education . . . .   _____

Childcare . . . .   _____

Clothing . . . .   _____

Personal grooming . . . .   _____

Entertainment (includes cable TV) . . . .   _____

Gifts (noncharitable) . . . .   _____

Charitable giving (includes church) . . . .   _____

Alimony . . . .   _____

Child support . . . .   _____

Contributions to savings . . . .   _____

Contributions to taxable investments . . . .   _____

Contributions to retirement plans . . . .   _____

Miscellaneous . . . .   _____

Total Monthly Expenses   _____

_____ − _____ = _____

Total income   Total expenses   Positive Cash Flow

Before writing a budget,
complete a family cash flow report.

When creating a budget, many people make the mistake of simply sitting down and making a list of expenses they need to have met and ascribing arbitrary numbers to each of those expenses. This is called creating a budget by going in through the back door—and it doesn't work. Properly creating a budget involves completing two different sheets or forms which are very similar to one another. The first one is a family cash-flow report. It tells you how much you're bringing home and what you're spending it on right now. The other is your budget. It represents to what and where your money will be going from now on.

Your family cash-flow report should serve as a complete inventory of where your money is being spent right now. (See "Cash Flow Chart" on page 34.) Make certain that you write down *every* category of expenditure, from "mortgage" or "rent," to "gasoline costs," to "miscellaneous" (the money your family spends on incidentals). Account for everything. The only way this will work is if you have a complete accounting of your monthly expenses. (To translate weekly expenses into monthly expenses, simply multiply your weekly expenses by 4.3.)

You may want to give yourself several days to create your cash-flow report. Often it is difficult to think of everything you regularly spend your money on each month. Keep the balance sheet handy, making sure to write down a new category every time you think of one. After a week or so, you should be able to account for everything.

TAKING ACTION

Construct a sound budget
based on your new lifestyle.

Once you have implemented the spending and, more importantly, the *attitude* changes we've talked about thus far, it's time to
construct a new spending plan for you and your family. It's important to realize, however, that a written budget is no more than
that. It's a written plan. If you are not committed within your
heart and mind to make the changes necessary to stick to the written plan, it will do you no good. To that end, I recommend that you
institute the changes we've already talked about and live them for a
while before you jump right in and put a budget together. In other
words, you might want to ease into the process. If you go straight
from living without a budget to trying to live *with* one, and do so
without first altering your heart and mind with respect to your
spending habits, your chances of success will be very small.

At the point you feel ready to construct the second half of
your written budget plan (the first half being the family financial
profile), sit down with your family and decide how much money
you're going to be allowed to spend in each expense area. In
truth, your written budget can look just the same as your written
family financial profile, the difference being that one will show
what you *have* been spending while the other will show what you
will spend from now on.

The first amounts you should fill in on the budget are those
which do not change from month to month or which you are obligated to pay each month, like the rent or mortgage payment and
the car payment. After that, you move on to everything else. You
and your family should engage in a serious discussion of each area

of expense to see where, if any, cuts can take place. Go through each area from the telephone bill, to the electric bill, to the grocery bill, and to everything in between. Settle on either a dollar amount or a percentage of income above which you will not spend.

Once you have finished this grand exercise, you will have your budget. In the beginning, it might be necessary to tape a large copy of it to the refrigerator to remind the family how important it is to the well-being of each member. After a while you can take it down, but keep it somewhere easily accessible.

TAKING ACTION

Plan according to your actual income, not what you expect it to be.

One common mistake made by many people who put a budget together is the mistake of wishful thinking. That is, they plan their budget, whole or in part, on the basis of income which is either irregular or not there at all. For instance, many people feel confident factoring in expected overtime revenue when determining their incomes—but that can be a mistake. Overtime income is hardly something upon which you can depend regularly. And even if it's available, you may not always want to take advantage of it; if you factor it in your monthly revenue, you may have no choice.

Additionally, some people are prone to assuming they will receive raises, bonuses, or windfalls of some sort, and will factor *those* into their budgets as well. Again, big mistake. Ignore those possible eventualities. (If they *do* occur, treat them as the extra revenue we spoke about earlier.) In the event of a raise, simply revise your budget to account for it—but don't account for it before it happens.

TAKING ACTION

Review your budget regularly, making adjustments as appropriate.

You should regard your budget as a living, breathing budget, one whose parameters should change as your financial circumstances change. If you get a raise, you should account for that change within your budget; likewise, if you pay off a credit-card bill entirely, be sure to eliminate that bill from your budget and reallocate the money that was going toward paying it off.

Do not, however, make the mistake of cheating on your budget under the pretense of "readjustment." Adjustments like the ones mentioned in the above paragraph should only be made in the event a substantive change to your financial profile occurs.

TAKING ACTION

If budgeting is especially difficult for you, consider the famous "envelope method."

The problem with written budgets is that they still present challenges for people who have an especially difficult time steeling themselves against temptation and making their spending habits as tangible as possible. A plan is just a plan; for it to work, it must be followed. Some people, despite their best efforts, can fail in their attempts to live in accordance with a sound written budget because of their inability to discipline their spending habits. These people may even have problems beyond those associated with a simple lack of discipline. However, it *is* possible to bridge the gap between the written plan and its implementation. One method of doing so is the famous "envelope method" of budgeting.

The envelope method is one example of "real" budgeting because it takes the budgeting from plan to action. With the envelope method, you convert your paychecks and other sources of family revenue to cash. Once that is done, you divide the cash into envelopes labeled with the various areas of expenses your family has. For example, if you have allocated $500 per month to groceries, put $500 of the cash into an envelope marked "groceries." If you have budgeted $50 per month to your Visa bill, put $50 in an envelope marked "Visa." As you can see, this forces you to physically allocate your money into these areas.

The envelope method of budgeting has a number of advantages. First of all, it bridges the gap between paper budgeting and real budgeting by its very nature. Additionally, the envelope method is a very simple budgeting system. Although some people might be insulted by its simplicity, remember, your family's financial well-being is a lot more important than your notions about pride. Also, use of the envelope method relieves the user of the responsibility of having to keep track of budgetary movements in writing. The money is just *there.*

As you might be able to see, however, there can be problems with utilizing the envelope method. First of all, using this method requires that you keep copious amounts of cash lying around the house. To limit the risk associated with this circumstance as much as possible, you would be well-advised to purchase a large, locking strongbox in which you can keep your envelopes. Keep *it* in a secure location within the house. Second, keeping cash available and readily accessible may be the wrong thing for a family who has difficulty disciplining themselves as to its proper, prudent use. Another problem with the envelope method is that if you have emptied one envelope but wish you had more money for its designated purpose, you might feel tempted to "borrow" from another envelope.

In truth, a lot of people who might otherwise wish to incorporate the envelope method of budgeting into their lives will likely be turned off at the hassle and risk of liquidating all of their revenue to cash and keeping it around the house. That's why this budgeting method is probably best-suited for those who don't make a lot of money. However, it can still be used by those with larger incomes, but it may have to be done in combination with other, more traditional methods of keeping money. For example, you could maintain a checking account for the purpose of paying such sizable obligations as mortgage or rent and the car payment. Beyond these, however, you could stick to the envelope method for the remainder of your bills.

The bottom line remains that, short of having a "mysterious force" take care of all your money concerns on your behalf, you must still do the work. This means that at some point, with all of the different budgeting methods at your disposal, you must be the one to make them work.

TAKING ACTION

Make living the budget the focus for your day-to-day financial management.

Make no mistake: Budgets work. For them to work, however, each member of your family must be dedicated to living the budget. This means that no decision should be made, no expenditure should be okayed without first ensuring that the family budget will not be compromised as a result. Although many parents are reluctant to burden children with family financial concerns, you should share them with your kids as much as possible to help youngsters understand what you're trying to accomplish and why it is so important. The entire family must embrace the budget and incorporate it into their day-to-day living. If this is not done, it is unlikely that budgeting will work for you—and you run the risk of spiraling downward into a pit of financial despair.

20 Ways
to Get Cash

If you don't have any money, then you would probably like someone to tell you how to get some . . . and fast! There are a lot of ways you can put more cash in your hands right away. I'll tell you right off that a few of the ideas we'll discuss here will require you to incur a measure of debt in order to access the money. Going into debt to put more money in your hands may sound like a case of borrowing from Peter to pay Paul, but if you are in a pretty severe cash-flow deficit situation, it may be necessary in the short term. Sometimes all you need to do is buy yourself some time—that's what some of these ideas are designed to do. Not all of them are intended to be permanent solutions to your problems. Many of the severe cash-flow problems that individuals experience are related to job loss, medical emergencies, and other out-of-the-blue events that make drastic demands on one's resources. Therefore, I don't feel that it's entirely inappropriate to propose some methods of cash procurement which involve taking on some debt.

Many of the ideas, however, are not dependent upon a willingness to incur debt in order for you to gain the cash. Some of them may appear to be commonsense suggestions, but others

are probably new to you. I've included many reasonable suggestions I feel are appropriate to let *you* decide which are best for
your personal circumstances.

TAKING ACTION

Access your company-sponsored retirement plan.

It's no secret that when you need to get your hands on some
money fast, some ways may be better than others with respect to
your personal circumstances. If you don't have a lot of money,
it's likely that you are already repaying debts such as car loans, a
mortgage, and credit cards. If this is your situation, it may not be
in your best interest to raise the cash in a fashion that requires
you to go deeper in debt. In this situation, you should first look
to sources you have available, even though you normally wouldn't
want to tap into them or don't think you should. A company retirement plan is a good example of one such source.

If you have worked somewhere that offers a retirement plan,
and you've been a participant in it for more than a few years, it's
quite possible you have accrued a few thousand dollars toward
your retirement. If you've worked there much longer, you might
have a substantial amount of money accumulated. It is usually
possible to get your hands on that money if you need to. It
should be said at this point that you should not approach the
withdrawal of money from your retirement plan lightly. First and
foremost, this is the fund upon which you'll primarily rely when
your working days come to an end. If you find yourself taking a lot
out of it, you might seriously injure your ability to enjoy a safe, secure retirement—one which frees you from worrying about

whether or not you'll have to take drastic measures such as selling your home in order to live.

All things considered, however, borrowing from your retirement plan can be superior to many other options. Because the money is your own, you aren't technically borrowing to get it. Furthermore, you may have a substantial sum available if you've been participating in the plan for a while. Furthermore, the interest you pay on the "loan" goes back to your own account. I know of one person who doesn't make very much money, but desperately needed some cash to pay for an unexpected emergency. Although her salary isn't very high, she had been an active participant in her company's retirement plan. This plan offered terrific investment options and had as its hallmark generous employer contributions. The upshot of this is that she was able to access a fair amount of money from her plan, and still have plenty leftover upon which she can continue building toward a comfortable retirement.

Finally, although the money is indeed yours, there is typically a measure of paperwork which must be completed before you receive your check from the company. The length of time between when you submit your paperwork and when you receive your check can be as long as a few weeks, so you should bear that in mind when you think about requesting the funds.

TAKING ACTION
Use your credit cards to get some cash in a heartbeat.

Some of you who read this principle may be thinking, *"Hey, wait a minute. I thought this guy was* against *people using their credit cards to obtain cash."* In general, I am. The interest rates charged on cash advances by some credit card issuers are obscene. And some competitively priced issuers will assess a separate, much-higher rate when the cards are used to obtain cash advances. All of this said, however, I recognize that you may need to get your hands on cash very quickly, and if you don't have many resources to begin with this may be one of your few viable options. This is one of the advantages of credit cards which cannot be denied. Because the standards for credit card issuance have become so relaxed over the years, the cards have come to represent a way for many people in dire economic straits to stave off doom while they look for work or search for more sensible, long-term solutions to their financial difficulties. I accept this, and understand the kind of help these cards can provide in that regard. However, because of the high cost of borrowing on credit cards, I continue to encourage people to look at them as tools of last resort.

Just about all credit cards, regardless of issuer, give you the opportunity to use them for cash advances at ATM machines. In many cases, local lenders will process your cash advance in their offices and you can walk out with the cash you need up to the limits of the cards. This may serve your needs better than using an ATM machine, which probably limits how much cash you can access at one time. If you have at least one card which has been issued by a local lender, you can get your hands on thousands of dollars in just a few minutes. This is the kind of timely access your situation may demand.

Another point to remember is that many card issuers supply checks which you can use to pay your obligations. These can be very helpful if you're in a situation where you cannot use your credit card outright to pay the bill. Checks don't burden you with the two-step process of using your cards to get cash, and then turning that cash into a money order to pay the debt. If you don't have any of these checks on hand, and you think that they may be just the ticket, contact the customer service division of your card issuer and ask for some. You can find the phone number on your monthly statement, as well as on the back of the card itself.

TAKING ACTION
Contact your creditors and arrange to skip your payments for a month.

If you're perpetually short of money, it's very likely that a large part of the reason has to do with the voluminous number of bills you face each month. If you're like most people, you have the usual two or three credit-card bills, the car payment, and maybe a few more installment loans covering various types of merchandise. Imagine how much money you'd have left over at the end of a given month if you were able to *skip* those payments just once. How much cash could you raise if you did that? $500? $1,000? More? Well, it may surprise you to learn that it is indeed possible to arrange to miss making a monthly payment on many of your bills. All it takes is a little planning.

The key to making this work is to contact your creditors *before* you miss making the payments. Do not skip any of your payments without asking first or assuming that it will be okay, because it won't be. As long as you are current on your payments, you should be able to talk many of your creditors into giving you at least a one-month "breather." The best way to do this is to get in contact by phone with a representative of the creditor company. Tell this person that you are anticipating a rough month, but that you'll be just fine if you could be allowed to skip your payment to the company just this one time. Also tell this person that you fully understand how important it is to maintain a quality credit record, and that you understand how important it is that his company gets back every penny of what he so generously extended to you. In other words, *empathize* with the company's position.

By mentioning these points and others like them, you demonstrate that you are a thoughtful consumer who understands the importance of repaying what has been borrowed. If you handle the situation correctly, you should find that at least a few of your creditors will work with you in this matter. I'm not saying that all of your creditors will go along with this, but you may be surprised at how many will—as long as you haven't had any bill-paying problems up to this point. I suggest that you follow up any affirmative answers to your query with a letter (sent "return receipt requested") to the person with whom you spoke; keep a copy for yourself. This will provide you with some insurance if the creditor changes his or her mind somewhere along the line.

Remember, you will not be able to use this strategy more than once in a long while, so be sure that this is the best option at that point in time when you decide you need money. You may find that some of your creditors will ask you to send something, perhaps the interest due on a particular payment. While this may not leave you with as much cash as you would like, it's certainly a lot better than having to send the whole payment. Take what you can get.

TAKING ACTION
Refinance your automobile.

If you own outright a later-model automobile, you should be able to get some money out of it. Banks and other lending institutions are usually quite amenable to making loans against anything of value. Automobiles are the kind of items they like to loan against because they are expensive and are in great demand by the public at large.

In general, a lender will loan you anywhere between 75 to 85% of the wholesale value of your vehicle. Some may loan more. For this to work, though, you must have title to the automobile, and it must be a newer-model car so that it has retained some real value (we're all familiar with the concept of depreciation). Go ahead and shop around among a variety of lenders. See how much each one will let you borrow and what kind of terms you can secure. As with any collateralized loan, your chances of getting the money should be excellent, because the lender is not simply depending on your character or bill-paying record to secure the loan. And, if you default, he gets your valuable automobile! Also be aware that the interest rates charged by lenders for these kinds of loans are not usually among the lowest. Nevertheless, if you need some quick cash, refinancing your car could be the way to go.

TAKING ACTION
Look to your whole life insurance policy to raise cash quickly.

I'm not a big fan of whole life insurance. I think it's way overpriced for what you get in addition to the basic insurance protection, which isn't much in my opinion. For example, one of the so-called perks of maintaining whole life insurance is that your policy builds cash value, a cash source you can borrow from under very liberal terms should you need money. It sounds great until you realize that cash value is simply a portion of your overpriced insurance premiums. Nevertheless, if you have this kind of policy and have held it for more than a few years, you probably have a bit of cash value built up which you can tap; if you've had the policy for many years, you may have quite a substantial amount of money accumulated in your cash value account. If you find yourself in need of some money, accessing your cash value account is not a bad way to go. Although I disagree philosophically with the existence of whole life insurance, and particularly with the artificial cash account it creates, my attitude is that if you already have the policy and you need some money, you might as well tap your cash value to get it.

When you take money out of your cash value account, it's considered a loan which you never have to repay. In other words, you can take as long as you want to make the payments (the interest charged is very low), and, in fact, you don't ever have to repay the money. However, you should be aware that the policy's death benefit will be reduced by the amount of cash value borrowed and still outstanding at the event of your death. If you borrow a lot and don't repay it, it may have some adverse consequences for your loved ones.

Overall, though, this is an excellent source of cash for you to tap. Again, I don't recommend that you go out and buy a whole life policy in order to build cash value (there are better ways to insure yourself and build a nest-egg at the same time). But, if you have the policy to begin with and you need some money right now, you might want to consider using it rather than borrowing from a lender under less convenient terms.

TAKING ACTION

Have money owed to you returned now.

If you're like most of us, you've been asked on occasion for a loan by a friend, relative, business acquaintance, or others.

Perhaps you even made the loan (Shakespeare's admonition "Neither a borrower, nor a lender be" notwithstanding!) because you had the money to do so. Now, however, your circumstances have changed; it's *you* who's in dire need of some cash—and quick! Is there any way you can have the amount of money you loaned returned to you more quickly so that you can extricate yourself from your current financial predicament? Very possibly, but it involves a little negotiation.

Although most creditors like to have borrowers continue to make payments over the regular course of their loans, they sometimes like to have the loans paid off early so that they have the opportunity to loan money again at higher rates. What we're talking about now is a variation of this idea because it's not likely that you're in need of cash because you want to loan it out again. Nevertheless, if you want the money back in your hands quickly, you might have to offer an incentive of some kind. One solid idea is to tell your borrower that if he can return the outstanding balance to you in a lump sum, you'll be willing to offer a discount.

For example, suppose someone owes you $2,000, and he's paying it off at $100 per month. At that rate, it will take you nearly two years to recoup your money. However, if you say to him (or her) that in exchange for a lump-sum payoff you'll knock the total owed down to $1,500 (a 25% savings for the borrower!) and call the whole deal square, you might well find him more receptive to paying the amount back in a lump sum.

Obviously, you have to find an amount which you find acceptable as a discount. Depending on your circumstances, you may well consider a 25% discount too generous. On the other hand, you might be willing to offer an even bigger discount in order to get your hands on something larger than $100 per month.

The most obvious problem with this method of raising cash is that it presupposes that you have made a loan to someone who is in the process of repaying it. Another thing to consider is that if this person was so hard up for money that he felt it necessary to borrow, he may not have the means to make a lump-sum payment of any kind. However, it never hurts to ask, and, although the return on your "investment" will be poor, employing this method of raising some cash quickly will *not* add to your debt burden. This is a feature many people find attractive in and of itself.

TAKING ACTION
Utilize the margin privilege in your brokerage account.

As I mentioned in the beginning of this chapter, one of the things you should always strive to do when trying to raise cash is to tap resources which are less sinister than a traditional lender. If you own shares of stock within a brokerage account, you may have found one.

Some of you who are in an especially difficult bind might think it's laughable to be talking about such things as stock portfolios and the like. After all, if you don't have any money, surely you don't own any stock. Well, that's not necessarily true. There are many people out there who have been bequeathed securities or have been given securities as gifts. Furthermore, remember our discussion in the beginning of the book about what really constitutes the condition of having no money. A lot of people who feel they're in that position are cash-poor but asset-rich. Admittedly, it is those people who will benefit the most from strategies such as this one.

If you own stock, you can usually borrow against it. The process is called "margin." Although most people use their margin privilege to purchase more stock, you can use it for any purpose which suits you. Margin rules (which are implemented and monitored by securities regulatory agencies) allow you to borrow up to half of the value of your stocks (as long as they are priced over $5 per share). This means that if you have a stock portfolio worth $10,000, you can borrow up to half of its value, or $5,000. Yes, you're still borrowing, but this is a case where you are essentially borrowing from yourself, so it's not as adversarial a proposition as borrowing from a lender oftentimes is.

There is one important fact about margining your stock portfolio that you should be cognizant of at all times. Remember when I said that when you margin you are essentially borrowing from yourself? Well, that's true, up to a point. You are borrowing against the value of your stock, but, as you know, the value of stock rises and falls in the market. If the value of your stock rises while your loan is outstanding, there's no problem. However, if it falls by more than 25% of its value, you'll get what is known as a "margin call." If you receive a margin call, your brokerage is telling you to deposit more money into your account because the 25%-plus drop in stock value means that they are now loaning you an amount in excess of 50% of the portfolio's value. If you can't physically deposit more money into the account, you can have the brokerage sell some shares of the stock to meet the call.

If you want to pursue the margin option, you will need to contact a broker at the brokerage where your stock is being held. It may take several days before you get a check. You'll find that margin loan rates are pretty reasonable, usually about 1 or 2 percentage points above the prime rate. As loans go, this kind is easy to take.

TAKING ACTION

If your property needs work but you have little equity, consider the FHA Title 1 Home Loan.

Although you can use a home equity loan for any number of purposes, a lot of people elect to use it for home-improvement projects. For many folks, it just seems natural to pull money out of the home in order to improve it. The *problem* with a home equity loan (or a second mortgage, for that matter) is that, as the name implies, you have to have some measure of equity in it to qualify. What if your home is in dire need of repair or improvement, though, and you have no equity? Is there any way you can get a home-improvement loan?

Yes, indeed! What I'm talking about is an FHA Title 1 home loan. The beauty of the Title 1 loan is that you don't have to have any equity in your home to qualify for it. Because it's insured by the federal government, it's a fairly easy loan to get. With a Title 1 loan, you can borrow up to $25,000 for home-improvement purposes.

During the application process, the lender will need to see a list of the improvements you plan to make with the money. They will likely need to see estimates from the various contractors you plan to use. If you borrow more than $7,500, the lender will inspect the work when it's done to ensure that you did what you said you were going to do. These monies are closely monitored. They *must* be used for home improvements.

Because you are borrowing money against a house with little or no equity, you need a good credit record to obtain the loan. This may make the Title 1 option prohibitive for those with a checkered credit history. Also, Title 1 loans aren't the cheapest in the world. The points and loan costs can be fairly high. (A point is an upfront fee charged by a lender; one point is equal to 1% of the principal amount of the loan.) However, this is one of those options where the advantages might offset the disadvantages to your satisfaction. Although you should be able to find several lenders locally who offer these loans, perhaps the best thing to do is to call the Department of Housing and Urban Development at 800-733-4663 or go to their website at www.hud.gov. Ask for a brochure describing this loan opportunity, as well as a list of lenders in your area who offer them.

TAKING ACTION
Hold a garage sale.

Most people know that garage sales exist and that lots of people have them. But how often do people think *they* should go to the trouble of putting one on? If you've lived in one place for a while, you have probably accumulated a lot of stuff. Many of these items may no longer have any real value or usefulness to you or your family. Frequently, you may even find yourself throwing away these perfectly good pieces of merchandise because you don't want to bother with them. If you need money, why not *sell* them? A garage sale may be the best way to dispose of unwanted household items that are functional. Such a sale can go a long way toward helping relieve any short-term financial strains you may be feeling at this time.

Admittedly, it's a lot easier to throw something out than it is to sell it, but which course of action is the smarter one? While setting up a garage sale takes a little time and effort, the payoff can be tremendous, especially if you've never had one before. If you're willing to part with a lot of what you have kicking around the house, you might well be able to raise all of the cash you need in the short-term. It's not unheard of for people to raise $1,000 or more from a single garage sale.

Your first step is to take an afternoon to make a list of everything that is worthy of being sold that you are willing to part with. Once you've determined a garage sale will be worth the time and trouble of setting it up, publicize the sale as much as possible. Many local newspapers and city papers have special sections in their Classified Ads just for announcing upcoming garage sales. Take advantage of that resource! Also be certain that you have posted signs and notices advertising the sale in surrounding areas. A lot of people make a hobby of attending garage sales. If you announce it right, you can have a substantial turnout. Weekends are the best times to hold a garage sale.

Perhaps my favorite reason for opting for the garage sale in cash-raising efforts is that money can be obtained without going into debt. As you've undoubtedly noticed, there are a lot of people and entities that are most willing to lend money for high rates of interest. To a great extent, that's always an option (unless you have terrible credit). If you have any options to raise your cash *without* going in debt, by all means use those first.

TAKING ACTION

Use your IRA funds free for two months.

Let me say at the outset of introducing this idea that I'm not overly keen on it. I'm including it because it's a viable avenue for people who are in dire need of short-term cash. There's a lot to pay attention to when utilizing this method. Let's go over everything you need to consider before deciding to raise your money in this manner.

If you have an IRA (Individual Retirement Account), you may take money out of it and keep it out for up to 60 days without incurring any kind of IRS penalty. However, in order to avoid the penalty you have to be able to redeposit what you removed within the 60-day time frame. Whatever you *don't* replace in that time will be assessed an IRS penalty of 10%, and that amount will be taxed as ordinary income. Although there are exceptions to the penalty rule, such as buying your first house, it's important to carefully evaluate what is allowed by contacting an IRS agent. The penalties are nasty enough, but they are not the most pressing reasons for replacing the money borrowed. The most important reason you need to pay back the money is because you are borrowing from your retirement—from the very thing which will allow you to enjoy a secure, comfortable lifestyle in your later years.

Because this option has a 60-day time frame, you don't have much to work with. This idea is probably best for those folks who are having a short-term cash crunch, but who fully expect to have additional sums coming in the very near future. Be advised that you may be one to two weeks away from seeing a check once you submit your IRA distribution request form to the trustee of your retirement plan. You need to do some advance planning before you see your money. If you think you may want to make an IRA withdrawal, contact a representative where your plan is located to find out precisely what steps you need to take.

TAKING ACTION

If you're a homeowner, consider a reverse annuity mortgage.

Reverse annuity mortgages have received a measure of publicity in recent years, but there are still a lot of people out there who have no idea what they are. With a reverse annuity mortgage, a person who owns his (or her) home outright can sell it back to the bank in a fashion that enables him to receive monthly payments. The reverse annuity mortgage is designed primarily to be used by older folks who may need some more money to live comfortably in their retirement.

An annuity is an arrangement whereby you receive regular payments for subsistence purposes for a length of time. Most annuities are facilitated as a result of an individual making an investment with an insurance company, and the insurance company making payouts from the invested monies to the individual once he or she retires. A mortgage, as you probably know, is an arrangement whereby property is pledged as security for a debt which is owed. With a reverse annuity mortgage, you receive monthly payments from the bank (rather than making them *to* the bank). The true source of the money is the equity in your house.

Reverse annuity mortgages can be excellent choices for more seasoned homeowners, particularly those who are in their 70s and older. Out of deference to life expectancy considerations, homeowners in their 70s can extract about twice as much from their homes as those in their early 60s. Once again, we are presented with an option for raising cash which does not require going into debt. This does not mean, however, that choosing a reverse annuity mortgage as your primary cash-raising method is a no-brainer decision.

First of all, remember that this money comes directly from the equity in your home. Once it's gone, that's it. Although it's not likely that you will outlive your annuity payments (your equity), it's a virtual certainty that the bank will end up with your home upon your death. This can be frustrating for people who expect to be able to leave their house (or at least the money from it) to their heirs.

There can also be fees and closing costs like those associated with the securing of any other type of mortgage. These fees can be expensive, so do your homework. Make sure you take the time to consult a knowledgeable tax advisor *before* you commit to the reverse annuity mortgage.

TAKING ACTION
Use a sale/lease-back mechanism to get some cash.

The following idea I'm going to propose may sound a little far-fetched at first, but it's entirely workable. In fact, large corporations, notably airlines, have used this strategy very successfully for years to give themselves an infusion of cash when necessary. What I'm talking about is the selling of an asset you own to a leasing company and the subsequent leasing back of the asset to use. Let's talk a bit more about how this works.

Let's say you own a computer that's worth a considerable sum of money and no one in the family uses it very often. If you're strapped for cash, it might be a good idea to contact a leasing company (there are lots of them around; just flip open the Yellow Pages) and ask if they'd be interested in buying it from you. If you still want to maintain use of the system, you could lease it right back. Using this sale/lease-back procedure, you can get cash fairly quickly and maintain the privilege of using the equipment as though you still owned it.

This mechanism can be used for a number of goods and types of property, but it may surprise you to learn that one type of property with which the strategy is used frequently is *real* property. It is not uncommon for a homeowner who is really strapped for cash to sell the house to an investor with the stipulation that he (the homeowner) gets to rent the property right back. This way, the homeowner comes up with the cash he needs, but is still able to reside in the home he has come to know and love. In some of these arrangements, the lease agreement stipulates that the homeowner (now the renter) will be able to buy the house back for a set price after a certain number of years.

There are a lot of real-estate investors out there who are looking for opportunities just like this. You can contact a real-estate agent who specializes in investment properties. He or she will know of several people who might be interested in this kind of arrangement. You can also run an ad in the real estate section of the newspaper that describes briefly what you're wanting to do. You can explain the rest to interested respondents.

This is a good example of how the use of some ingenuity can help extricate you from a cash crunch. You may find that if you aren't willing to go into debt in order to raise some money, then you may have to start thinking somewhat unconventionally in order to get what you want.

TAKING ACTION

Need some cash?
How about a second mortgage?

I don't know if this is the most common method by which homeowners who need money get it, but it has to rank right up there near the top of the list. Homes are such valuable assets that it's tough not to consider them when you need a boost of cash. If you've owned the home for quite a while, you probably have built up a fair amount of equity. As a result, you might be able to access a tremendous amount of cash—as much as tens of thousands of dollars! As a general rule, lenders will only loan up to 80% of the property's value. This means that if your property is worth $100,000 and you owe $60,000 on your first mortgage, you will be able to borrow up to $20,000 additionally. (The formula: Multiply your current property value by .80, then subtract the amount remaining on your first mortgage.)

Your home can be a great source of money, but be careful when seeking a second mortgage. First of all, you are pledging your home as collateral for your loan. This means that if you cannot make the payments, you will lose it. It's that simple. For this reason, I encourage people who are considering a second mortgage to be as judicious as possible when deciding on how much to borrow. *Do not borrow any more than you absolutely need.* By keeping the amount as low as possible, you keep your repayment burden as low as possible and keep your risk as low as possible. Additionally, you will be faced with assorted fees and closing costs, so be sure to shop around to keep those amounts low. Also shop around to find the lowest interest rate.

By the way, if you expect to need the money for several different purposes over an extended period of time, you might want to consider a home equity loan. The chief difference between a second mortgage and a home equity loan is that with the home equity loan you're receiving a line of credit you can access whenever you need it. With the second mortgage you receive the money all at once and are charged interest right away. Have a firm handle on your reasons for borrowing, including the time parameters at your disposal, in order to ensure that you get the best deal.

TAKING ACTION
Take your vacation money
...and run!

Most companies have some kind of benefits package available to employees, and the cornerstones of these packages are usually health care and vacation time. Now, there's not much of a chance that you'll be able to tap your health insurance for any cash (at least no way of which I'm aware), but if you have some vacation time accrued, you might be able to trade those days for some valuable, badly needed dollars. Many employers permit their employees to cash in their vacation days every so often and take the money. This can be a great source of cash if the choice is available to you. For example, if you earn $300 per week and have accrued two weeks' worth of vacation, you may be able to opt to forgo the actual vacation and take the money equivalent instead—in this case, two weeks of pay ($600).

This can be a great option for people who are reluctant to go deeper in debt than they currently are. However, as with all of these methods of raising cash, the person electing this particular method must accept a measure of trade-off. Here, the trade-off is that you must, of course, part with valuable vacation time that you may need every bit as much as the money! All in all, this is probably one of the better ways to get money because it asks the least of you in return. Keep in mind the prospective loss of the vacation time. As a compromise to yourself, you might consider cashing in just a portion of the days available (say one week's worth instead of two) and keeping the balance for a real vacation. That's up to you, but be sure of your plans before you commit to this course of action.

TAKING ACTION
Adjust your withholding.

If you are an employee (not self-employed), the accounting department of the company you work for withholds a portion of your paycheck for federal income tax purposes. The amount withheld is based primarily on the number of exemptions you declared on the W-4 form you filled out when you started working there. The W-4 form instructions offer guidelines as to how it should be filled out, but one of the little secrets of the withholding election procedure is that *you* can decide how much money you want withheld by deciding how many exemptions you want to declare. You can, for instance, go down to your accounting department and fill out a new W-4, claiming more exemptions than you did when you first started. The result of this is that your take-home amount will be greater. Depending on the number of exemptions you declared when you started and the number you claim now, you might well give yourself an instant raise of a few hundred dollars each month. If you don't make a lot right now, the difference will not be that substantial, but everything's relative. As long as the instant raise you give yourself makes a substantial, positive impact on your take-home pay, then the adjustment will have served its purpose.

There are a couple of other points which should be mentioned before we leave this idea and move on to others. First, getting an increase in your weekly paycheck, regardless of how quickly it comes, may not give you as much money as you're looking to raise. That's why this option is not as effective in raising cash quickly, but is more a method to help ease your week-to-week or month-to-month budget strain. The chief advantage of this method is that the trade-off might be less taxing than the other options. You don't need to part with anything, and you don't need to go into debt. (I suppose the fact that you can't raise as much money as quickly is a disadvantage of this method.)

Also, you need to be aware of how making this adjustment will affect you at income-tax time. If you are used to receiving a substantial refund each year, you will find that it will be much smaller. In fact you may end up owing Uncle Sam come April 15. As long as you're prepared to pay a tax bill (and as long as it's not too substantial), cutting your withholding so that you pocket more money throughout the year is a more-than-acceptable way to go.

TAKING ACTION
Recoup deposits and save money by canceling or cashing in goods and services.

When you moved to your present location, did the telephone company ask you to pay a deposit before it initiated your service?

What about your utility company? I know that the deposits asked by these companies can be well into the hundreds of dollars. Did you have to pay, by chance? What about your gas supplier? Cable television? The fact is, there are many service providers out there who demand deposits of one size or another from customers before they will "turn on the juice," as it were.

If you have been a customer of service providers for at least a year, and have been making your payments faithfully and timely, why not contact them to see if they would be willing to return your deposits? Remember, the reason you pay deposits to begin with is to give the providers some protection if you turn out to be a problematic bill payer. If you've been making the payments without difficulty for a while, you may well have earned the right to have some or all of your deposit returned. I know of many service providers that actually return the deposit to the customer automatically after a certain period of time (as long as the payment record has been good).

You may find that some of these folks will turn you down. Rules governing the collection of such deposits are typically governed by state laws, so there's every reason to believe that if they've asked for the money and are keeping it, then it's because they have the right to do so. However, if you contact the customer service department of each of these organizations and plead your case (emphasizing, of course, your outstanding payment record), you may find a few receptive ears. Most companies will do their best to keep customers as happy as possible—even if the company in question has somewhat of a monopoly in your area regarding the designated service.

A distant cousin to this method of raising some cash is the idea of canceling various subscriptions and memberships to magazines, clubs, and so forth that you don't use very much. Lots of people find themselves signing up and purchasing subscriptions to things which they don't really use that much, but never get around to canceling. Well . . . get around to it! Take an inventory of the things you purchase on an ongoing basis, but which you don't seem to use very often (if at all). Make a point of sitting down and canceling them. This may not seem like something that will be very helpful at first, but if you are truly starved for cash, this can only help.

TAKING ACTION

Head to the pawnshop
with some of your goodies.

A lot of people continue to look at pawnshops these days as being nasty little places where only ne'er-do-wells are willing to be seen. While many pawnshops may indeed fit the stereotype, many do not. Because decent, well-educated people are having such a tough time making ends meet, pawnshops have become as much an opportunity for financial assistance for them as for anyone else . . . why not you, too?

Very simply, a pawnshop loans you money against the value of something you give as collateral. If you bring them a $1,000 stereo system, the pawnshop will loan you some money which represents a portion of the value of the stereo. You and the pawnbroker work out terms over which the loan is to be repaid and by when you must reclaim your merchandise.

If you don't pay off the loan and reclaim your property within the agreed-upon time frame, the pawnshop then has the right (which it invariably exercises) to sell the property to the general public.

Notice that a little earlier I mentioned that the pawnbroker will loan you "a portion" of the value of the item you offer as collateral. Pawnshops will generally lend only between one-quarter to one-half of the value of the item being pawned. And, while that may seem unfair, remember that the pawnbroker is in business to make money. If he loans you 100% of the value of the collateral and you never make any payments, the best that he could expect to do is break even. By loaning only a small portion of the item's value, he is giving himself some protection. He adds to that protection a little further by charging fairly outrageous rates of interest on the loan, much higher than you'll ever pay to more conventional lenders.

The big advantage to using a pawnshop for someone in need of money is that he can get it quickly. The whole transaction takes place in minutes, and you generally receive your loan in cash. Also, although you are receiving a loan, it's secured by collateral which is probably nonessential to you. This means your whole life will not likely be turned upside down if you have problems paying the money back. Obviously, there are some disadvantages to going the pawnshop route, including the small portion of your collateral's value which you receive and the high rates of interest charged. All in all, though, this method of raising quick cash is about as user-friendly as any.

TAKING ACTION

Purchase, repair, and resell merchandise.

Are you at all handy with tools? If so, it may be a lot easier to raise some cash than you currently think. A growing number of people are finding great opportunities by purchasing big-ticket items in need of refurbishment at dirt-cheap prices, doing the needed work, and reselling the stuff for many times what they paid for it. It could be anything from cars down to small TV sets. Cars are viable choices. Many times you don't need a lot of automotive mechanical knowledge to make the plan work. For example, a lot of cars in otherwise decent condition will be offered to the public for a diminished price because of the great amount of cosmetic work needed to bring the car back up to speed (pardon the pun). If you are into detailing at all and are handy enough to replace mirrors and the like, it's possible to strike gold through these kinds of efforts. Obviously, you don't need to limit yourself to autos. There are all kinds of things out there which lend themselves to this kind of work. I know of someone who has done a good job making a sideline business out of fixing and reselling machines such as lawn mowers and chain saws. These kinds of items are especially suitable for people without much money because they don't cost a lot to purchase at the outset.

The most obvious problem with this method of raising money is that it adheres to the classic maxim "it takes money to make money." In other words, you must have a little money to get started—and if you're reading this book, you may not have any (or enough). Still, if you are able to use a number of the strategies in this book together, you may save enough money to begin this venture.

There is one caution regarding this option. If you engage in this money-raising procedure with some regularity, the IRS could take the position that you are a business and that you must pay taxes on what you earn—something you want to avoid unless you're ready for the responsibilities of a home-based business. Furthermore, if you are judged to be a business, you may have to contend with a variety of local ordinances regarding running a business in general and the kind of business you're running in particular. Do your homework.

Factor your receivables to raise some money.

If you're a business owner, you probably have unpaid receivables in your possession from time to time. (Receivables are accounts with outstanding balances.) If you have a lot of them and you're strapped for cash, you may want to consider factoring your receivables. When you factor your receivables, you sell them off at a discount for cash. You may sell them off to an investor or group of investors or to a bank. One common way receivables are used by businesses to raise cash is to use them as collateral against a loan for the needed funds. There are, in fact, lenders out there who specialize in making loans against receivables. You can find them in the Yellow Pages under the heading "Factors." Depending on the status of your receivables (how old they are, how much they are worth), you may decide that selling them at a discount is preferable to getting a loan against them for their full value. Only you can make that decision. Nevertheless, for business owners who are in need of a quick infusion of cash for their enterprises, this can be a great way to get it.

As you can see, this strategy is not much different than the strategy of having the money owed to you repaid more quickly in exchange for a discount. The basic underlying mechanism which makes these strategies work is very common: The choice between getting some of what you're owed now or all of what you're owed later. It may not seem fair that these decisions have to be made in the first place. As long as people enter into financial arrangements with one another, these decisions will exist.

TAKING ACTION
As a last resort, sell your home.

I debated with myself long and hard before including this cash-raising idea. After all, it's not easy to recommend to anyone that the best solution to their financial troubles is for them to sell their house. But you know what? Sometimes it is. Let's face it: If you find yourself consistently short of cash, there's a reason for it. One aspect of the problem likely has to do with the fact that you're not making enough money, but the truth is that you always have the capacity to live within your means. If you're not doing that, you really have a problem.

If you are able to perform an objective self-assessment on your financial situation, you may find that you have some big impediments to living within your means. How big is your mortgage? How much of your monthly income does it consume? Unfortunately, many people buy into the notion that is put forth by real-estate brokers. They claim that the prospective home buyer can afford to make a payment which represents as much as 29% of his or her gross monthly income. Maybe that figure was accurate at one time, but in this day and age when two car payments and a bevy of monthly credit-card payments per household are common, it seems awfully dangerous to allocate 30% of your monthly income to your mortgage. The truth is, though, that some people buy houses which make more of a demand than *that* on their monthly paycheck. If you just can't hack your house payment along with your other responsibilities each month, it may be time to think about dumping your house payment (or at least lowering it). If you're going to do this, you should do so *before* foreclosure ever becomes an issue. Use your abilities to spot trouble before it starts, and to make corrective changes accordingly. I know that selling your home as a way to raise money seems unthinkable, but think about this: If you allow yourself to fall deeper and deeper into trouble, you may soon find yourself in foreclosure proceedings. Then you'll lose your home, the equity you've built up in it, and your good credit record.

Raising money in emergencies is not a comfortable position to be in. These ideas for raising cash, most of which should be viewed as a last resort, are very practical. It goes without saying (but I will say it anyway) that if you find yourself using these ideas for any extended period of time, you are not truly dealing with the root problem of your financial circumstances. I hope this chapter has served as an emergency parachute for those who feel their financial circumstances are plummeting fast. I am confident that the strategies contained in this chapter, as extreme as some may be, are far superior options than personal bankruptcy.

Fighting Back with Smart Banking

Money is the currency of choice, nowadays, and has been ever since the inception of so-called modern times. Long gone are the days when businesspeople and artisans would exchange services or products as compensation for one another's labors. But where do you keep all of this money? It's certainly not convenient (or safe!) for employers to deliver pay to employees in the form of cash. And bill paying would be a substantial hassle for each of us if we were without the opportunity to pay said bills with checks. Yes, it's difficult to get by in this day and age without banks. Plus, if no one were depositing money anywhere, where would we go for loans (the real way banks make money)? No, the truth of the matter is that we *must* go to banks, and because of that we are somewhat at their collective mercy.

Ever-Increasing Fees

We are told that banks need us, so consequently we should be bold and demanding when applying for loans. After all, that's how banks *make* the bulk of their money—by giving loans and charging interest (usually much more than they pay to depositors). That sounds okay, but if that's true, how come banks get away with charging us ridiculous fees for ridiculous things? After all, if they need us more than we need them, surely they should be bending over backward to make certain we are as delighted as possible with them at all times. We all know, however, that such is not the case.

Banks seem to take no displeasure whatsoever from nickel-and-diming us at every turn. One reason more pronounced in recent years, which seems to have given them even more of a license to do this than what they apparently felt they had already, is the disconcerting trend toward mergers and consolidations. It seems as though smaller, more regional banks (you know, the ones that historically offered "the little guy" a better deal) are continually being gobbled up by larger banks with more nationwide and worldwide ties. The resulting shrinkage in the number of truly separate banking institutions has resulted in (surprise!) an increase in banking costs overall.

Should we be shocked at this? After all, you don't need a degree in economics to know that a reduction in competition between producers of like services or products means that consumers have less to choose from, so costs of said services or products will rise. That principle is as applicable to the banking industry as it is to anything else. Interestingly, I have actually heard banking honchos who work for larger institutions say that such mergers are better for the consumers. Then they go on to give a bizarre explanation as to why that is. Don't believe them. If your local bank turns into one of the giants you see advertised on television constantly nowadays, chances are pretty good that you'll be paying more in fees very shortly.

Consequently, if you are someone who hasn't very much money at all, and certainly none to waste, you will want to be as well-armed as possible in order to properly fight the banking wars. You may not realize it, but there are several steps you can take to ensure that you are not overpaying for the bank privileges that all of us once viewed as being free forever. One thing I will tell you at the outset is that if you expect to win this battle, be prepared to do two things in large quantities: shop around and be assertive. Many people are reluctant to do either. The former, because the process of shopping around takes time, and time is something we don't like to use much of when doing things which don't provide immediate, pleasurable gratification. The latter, because it goes against the inclination of most of us to be non-controversial and nonadversarial. Nevertheless, if you are reading this book for necessity's sake, don't worry so much about what others (besides your family members) think of you. Simply be concerned with turning your life around.

TAKING ACTION
Whenever possible, choose to do your banking at credit unions instead of banks.

Have you ever heard of a credit union? Probably. Do you know what a credit union is? Maybe not. Credit unions are financial institutions which exist for the benefit of particular groups of people. Credit unions for teachers are pretty common, as are credit unions for a variety of other professions, groups, and organizations. The best thing about credit unions is that they are run for the benefit of their members. Credit unions are not plagued by that tug-of-war match which so often works to the detriment of bank depositors. You see, when deciding what to pay on deposits and what to charge for loans, banks must concern themselves with the business of making money for their shareholders. Credit unions face no such quandary. As a result, the terms found at credit unions are usually much better than those found at more traditional financial institutions. In general, credit unions charge less for loans and pay more on deposits. You'll find that the nickel-and-dime service charges that all banks seem to charge these days are either much lower or completely nonexistent at credit unions. Even minimum balance requirements on checking accounts are much more user-friendly at credit unions. If you're watching your pennies, you will undoubtedly find credit unions to be much more to your liking than banks.

To belong to some credit unions, you have to first belong to a group or to an organization which has a credit union set up in its behalf. These credit unions exist for the benefit of employees of certain companies, government agencies, nonprofit institutions, labor unions, and trade associations. However today there are "community" credit unions anyone can belong to. In order to find out if you are eligible to join a credit union or to find one in your area, contact the Credit Union National Association (800-358-5710).

One more thing. Before you sign up at a credit union, make sure that your account(s) will be insured by the National Credit Union Association (NCUA). There are a few privately insured credit unions out there which do not offer the same protection to your money as that which is offered by the NCUA, so be sure to avoid them.

TAKING ACTION

Shop for a checking account with the minimum balance calculated by the average daily balance method.

Unfortunately, there aren't many banks which offer no-minimum checking. There may be a few, but those that do usually do so as part of a promotional offer designed to get people to open accounts. It is pretty much a given that you'll be faced with the likelihood of paying a service charge if your account drops below the designated minimum level during the course of a given month. This problem is often especially relevant if you're having pronounced money problems. It then becomes important to scrutinize every aspect of your banking relationship to ensure that you're not paying out in the form of fees any more than is absolutely necessary. A good place to start is your checking account.

Beyond knowing what the raw-dollar figure is below which your checking account balance may not slip without the assessment of a fee, you also need to know *how* the minimum balance requirement is calculated and enforced. Avoid maintaining your checking account at a bank that hits you with a monthly fee (I call it a penalty) if your account balance drops below the minimum for even one day. Find a bank where the *average daily balance* method is used to calculate the minimum. This means that your account is not assessed the penalty unless its *average* balance for the entire month drops below the minimum standard. This is a much more consumer-friendly way to arrive at the figure, as it will save someone who's usually teetering at the brink of the minimum amount a lot in service charges over the course of the year.

TAKING ACTION
Negotiate to get free checking privileges.

I believe that the power of negotiation is vastly underused and underrated. Most people seem willing to put up with whatever merchants throw at them, just to keep from raising a fuss or causing a scene. Has it ever dawned on you that if you don't like the price of something, simply ask for one that is lower? Sure, you'll be turned down quite a bit, maybe almost all the time. However, if you're persistent you'll find that the few times you are successful can make up for all those times you aren't.

The best way to begin your quest to get something you want from a merchant (yes, even a banker) is to ask first. Simply asking for something you want may be more effective than you ever imagined. The reason most people don't think to do it, however, is because they automatically assume they'll be turned down. If you are, fine; now you must turn to the fine art of negotiation for assistance. Negotiation can be quite effective if you're shopping banks. In the minds of most consumers, bank fees are nonnegotiable; they are what they are, and that's it. Well, the truth is, that's *not* it. If you want free checking, ask for it. If you want a better credit card rate, ask for it. Many individuals who listen to my radio show have gone into their banks and asked for a lower interest rate on their credit cards and guess what? They were given it.

You can *negotiate* for free checking. How? Well, one good way is to offer to have your paycheck deposited directly into your account at that institution. Banks love direct deposit, because it relieves them of the paperwork associated with manual deposits. Furthermore, the bank receives assurance (more or less) that it will be receiving your money on a regular basis. The truth is, you may want to have your paycheck direct-deposited anyway, because doing so probably means less hassle for you. But I would resist doing so until you've tested on the "open market" the value of your willingness to have direct deposit.

You might also want to consider asking for free checking on a number of other bases. For example, if you're in the market for a loan, perhaps you could agree to give your loan business to the bank if they were willing to give you free checking. (To keep from committing to a loan rate which is excessive, however, you should make this offer with the stipulation that you will shop out your loan application elsewhere. Then *if* this institution is among the lowest, you'd be willing to place it there.) Additionally, you could guarantee that your spouse or some other person you know will move *his or her* money to the bank in exchange for the free checking (if you can make such a claim). The point is that there are a lot of ways to get a better deal at your bank. The key lies in not giving anything away without first seeing if you can get something in return.

TAKING ACTION

Don't buy your checks from the bank.

If you don't have much money, you seek every opportunity available to save as much as possible. That being the case, you may want to consider another idea which relates to saving money on your checking. However, in this case, I'm not talking about the account—I'm talking about the checks themselves!

The vast majority of people believe that if they have a checking account located at a particular bank, then they must purchase their checks from that same bank. It's just not true. There's nothing about your check which has to come directly from the bank where your account is located. Again, we have encountered another banking profit center which leaves you, the little guy, with less in your pocket when it's all said and done. The fact is, you can purchase your checks on your own, direct from a printer. There are a growing number of check printers who market their services directly to the public, and you can save yourself a bunch of money by traveling this route. How much did your last batch of 200 checks cost? $20? $25? By ordering directly from the printer, you can cut that cost in half or more—and you can still get designer checks which reflect your own personality (if that's important to you). There are several companies that market checks directly to consumers. The following are some names of check-printing services, along with their telephone numbers, to get you started.

Image Checks	800-562-8768
Designer Checks	800-239-9222
Checks in the Mail	800-733-4443

TAKING ACTION

If your ATM privileges are not free, leave your bank.

If you think I'm kidding, think again. There's just no reason for you to do business at a bank which insists on charging its customers to use their automated teller machine. In general, most banks will allow its *customers* to use its ATMs for free. If your bank does not allow that, you need to find another place to do your banking. Before you make the decision to leave, talk to the customer service representative at your bank and see if there's any way you can get free ATM privileges. If not, move on. For people who do not have much money, paying for ATM privileges at the bank where you do business is an incredibly needless waste of money.

TAKING ACTION
Avoid using
the ATMs of other banks.

Do you want to see what little money you have slip through your fingers more quickly than it is already? Make a habit of using the ATMs which belong to other banks. The ATMs of banks and other organizations to which you don't belong or don't receive free usage of should be regarded as absolutely off limits. Whenever you use the ATMs of banks to which you don't belong, it is not uncommon to find yourself paying $1.50 to $2.00 for each transaction. ATMs are great innovations, and the ease and simplicity they provide in our day-to-day existence are tough to overemphasize. Nonetheless, if you make a habit of using the wrong ATMs you will find yourself left with even less money than you have currently.

TAKING ACTION
Don't buy your investment products
from the bank.

As time goes by, banks seem to be increasingly privileged to sell financial products which were once off-limits to them. Many banks, which at one time were restricted to offering interest-bearing savings and checking vehicles, may now offer mutual funds, stocks, and various insurance products. The hallmark of this idea from the banks' point of view is that with all of these financial customers coming into the lobby on a daily basis, it would make sense for these folks to make that extra leap and do all of their financial business at the institution. Simplicity and ease are the watchwords here, and many bank customers have responded quite favorably (again, from the banks' point of view).

The truth is, however, that if you are concerned with saving money, you don't want to purchase your investment or insurance products from your bank. First of all, any of these instruments sold through a bank will usually end up costing you more—and it can be a lot more. There are countless numbers of ways to save money on insurance, but you probably won't hear any of them from your banker. Many banks now have brokerage services through which you can purchase individual stocks, but there are much less expensive ways to do the same thing elsewhere. On the subject of mutual funds, you'll find that because you're buying them through an agent when you buy them at the bank, you pay a commission. There is never any reason to pay a commission in order to access a high-quality mutual fund. (This will be covered in some depth in the chapter "Become an Investor for $50 a Month.") Bank mutual funds will probably cost you anywhere from 4% to 8% in commissions, an expenditure of your money which is nothing short of a total waste.

The keys to winning at purchasing investment products on a shoestring budget are to purchase them without paying a commission (or a very, very low commission) and to invest very small sums of money into them. Mutual funds and other financial products sold by banks rarely ever offer those advantages, so it is in your best interests to keep your utilitarian banking needs separate from your investment needs at all times.

TAKING ACTION
Don't avoid checking accounts in favor of money orders.

Very often, people who operate with very little cash flow find that it makes more sense to keep their funds available in cash. They simply purchase money orders when it comes time to pay bills. While I admit that it may seem rather senseless for someone who is perpetually broke to keep a checking account, the truth is that he or she will usually be better off by doing so when all is said and done. Have you seen the price of money orders lately? A lot of places that once dispensed them for a few cents have chosen to regard them as profit centers and have increased the prices of these simple financial instruments into the range of a few dollars. If you're like most of us, you probably have a bunch of bills to pay each month (which is probably the real reason you're broke, anyway). So, although it may not seem on the surface like a smart idea for you to maintain a checking account, the truth is that money orders will cost you a lot more in the long run. The only acceptable reason for opting for the money-order route as opposed to maintaining the checking account would be if you always have a difficult time keeping the minimum monthly balance in your account and you're hit with charges from your bank on a regular basis. As I said earlier, no-minimum checking accounts do exist; you may have to be somewhat persistent in your search for them, but they are out there.

TAKING ACTION
Don't pay for overdraft protection.

One bank option which is attractive to many people who have money troubles is overdraft protection. The purpose of overdraft protection is to keep you from bouncing checks. With overdraft protection, you can write checks for more money than you have in the bank, and your overdraft credit line will protect you for the difference. For people who are constantly "on the line" when it comes to their bills, the appeal of maintaining overdraft protection is obvious.

The problem with overdraft protection is that once you know it's there, it becomes much easier to rely on. Lots of people regularly dip into their overdraft credit line to pay their bills, thereby incurring a double-whammy for themselves: Not only must they make up the difference, but they now owe interest on what they borrowed by using the overdraft credit line. (You didn't think overdraft protection was free, did you?) In fact, the interest charged on overdraft credit lines can be among the highest rates you'll pay to borrow anywhere. So avoid accessing it whenever possible.

Keep more of your money in your own pocket, and forgo the overdraft protection. Sure, this will mean that you'll have to pay very close attention to your financial inflow and outflow, but so what? You should be doing that anyway. If you find that you're broke at the end of every month, the last thing you should be doing is utilizing any kind of overdraft protection which can cost you an arm and a leg.

There's another problem with having overdraft protection that works to hurt the financially strapped consumer, albeit in a more subtle fashion. If you're having a difficult time living within your means, there's a good chance that part of your problem has to do with a lack of self-discipline. I talked about this extensively in the chapter "Financial Freedom on a Budget," but it bears mentioning here as well. As long as you have overdraft protection, you will not maintain the necessary vigilance and have the sense of urgency about your bank account that you otherwise would. In other words, your overdraft protection becomes one more crutch upon which you lean to keep from having to extricate yourself from adverse financial situations.

Make the commitment *today* to drop the overdraft protection. Resolve to take better care of your checking account—saving yourself money now and in the future.

TAKING ACTION

Aggressively pursue your bank when you disagree with a charge or fee.

It is in the nature of most people, especially Christians, to be nonadversarial. Most people would rather pay a charge they disagree with or put up with shoddy service than make a fuss or have an otherwise unpleasant interaction with a merchant or service provider. While I understand the desire to keep one's associations and interactions as pleasant as possible, there comes a time when your rights (even your perceived rights) as a consumer should supersede your concerns about having a negative dialogue with someone who has wronged you in the marketplace.

I'm talking about the idea of calling your bank to discuss an assessed fee with which you disagree or a policy that you don't like (especially if it takes money out of your quickly depleting billfold). Banks seem to enjoy an exalted stature within our society, especially from the vantage point of the consumer. While many of us would be agreeable to complaining to a typical retail merchant about poor service or unreasonable fees or costs, it seems as though we shy away from doing the same thing when it comes to banks. Banks do seem to have a lot of influence over us. After all, we keep our money in banks, and when we need to purchase a sizable item of value (for example, a car or house) we often head to the bank to ask for a loan. Perhaps we're afraid that if we make the bank angry, it will make our money disappear somehow, or we won't ever have a prayer of being approved for a badly needed loan. The worst thing we can do is to let *any* business—including banks—make us feel powerless in their presence. If your bank has charged a fee that you disagree with, then by all means speak up!

When I say you should challenge the bank over costs with which you disagree, I'm not just referring to erroneous charges to your account (that you would argue those should go without saying). I'm also talking about ridiculous nickel-and-dime fees and charges which banks, in their pronounced arrogance, feel privileged to charge at our expense. I know of one bank, for example, which actually charges customers when they bring rolls of change in to exchange for paper money! You may be aware of the trend on the part of banks to "encourage" customers to do all of their banking at ATMs by charging customers every time they walk into the bank and do their business with a human teller. Some of these fees are as high as $5! There's more. Many banks are now starting to assess fees for customers who make telephone inquiries regarding their accounts. In this case, the bank usually grants a certain number of free inquiries during each statement period (how nice of them), but charge for every one over that maximum…and the number of free calls allowed is not very high.

One of my "favorite" charges is the one assessed when *someone else* bounces a check written to you. That's right! A lot of banks will charge *you* a fee if you deposit a check which was written on insufficient funds. I've seen these fees reach as high as $20 per episode. It is absolutely unconscionable that a bank would charge the depositor (clearly the victim) for the sins of the check writer, but it often does.

One of my employees told me not long ago about the crazy charges at his bank. He mentioned one which struck me as being particularly unreasonable. His bank assesses a fee if the depositor uses one of the deposit slips made available in the bank lobby instead of using the slips from his checkbook! Another one of my employees told me that when he reordered checks from his bank which were subsequently lost in the mail, he was told that if he wanted to have the checks canceled for security reasons he'd have to pay a $15 charge.

Perhaps the most offensive kinds of bank charges to be found are those like the one just mentioned, where the *depositor* is charged anything. It's bad enough when we're charged for taking money *out* of the bank; why should one who is trying to put money *into* the bank be charged for doing so?

You should get the picture by now: Bank fees are out of control. Sometime in the last 10 to 15 years, banks decided that their very own depositors—the people on whom they depend to stay in business—should be fleeced in order to fill the banks' coffers even higher. Banks try to tell us how much it costs to do business, but don't buy it. A recent survey showed that banks collect $25 in fees for every $1 of bounced checks. Do you think they're just breaking even on that deal?

One of the positive signs I've noticed in all of this is that banks will waive a lot of these fees if you simply ask. For example, remember the employee I mentioned who was faced with paying to have his lost checks canceled? It turns out that he was able to get that fee waived by calling the customer service department of his bank. Studies show that banks waive millions of dollars in fees every single year. (I must admit that I'm somewhat disillusioned. After all, if these guys are so magnanimous about waiving these fees, what does that tell you about how necessary these fees are to cover bank costs? You don't think the bank would waive these fees if they were losing money, do you?)

Face it, folks. When it comes to bank fees, it's us against them. Be aggressive about pursuing your bank if you're facing charges which you deem unreasonable. If your bank tells you that a charge is "standard," or that it's "bank policy" to assess the fee, call them on it. The growing number of bank mergers and consolidations have already gone a long way toward stifling competition (and increasing your costs), so you must be willing to steel yourself to the task of arguing and lodging complaints if you want some relief.

TAKING ACTION
Check out convenience options.

Most financial institutions now allow you to use the internet to check on account information such as balances, cleared checks, deposits, withdrawals, interest information, loan information, and tax information. You can also transfer money between accounts, have a check issued to you, order checks, and even get loan estimates. Ideally these services should be offered at no charge or for a nominal fee.

Another featured service at most financial institutions is bill-paying. For a fee you can set up an online account that lets you pay bills through the bank. This works one of two ways. If the payee allows electronic payments, the bank service transfers the money to the payee's account. If the payee doesn't accept electronic transfers, the service will write and mail a check to the payee's account. But remember, this convenience costs money. If it's cheaper for you to write your own checks, by all means do so and save money!

Check with your local banks to see if they offer these convenient services and more. For a list of online banks you can check out my website at www.christianmoney.com.

Protecting Your Family's Future Through Insurance

Insurance remains the quintessential example of something you should be willing to purchase in reasonable quantities, but hope you never have to use. Sadly, many people choose to go without even the most necessary financial coverages because they believe they can't afford them. Their rationale, however, goes beyond a question of simple affordability. Some people believe that as long as they're careful, they'll never need insurance. *This* is the quintessential example of dangerous thinking. This chapter is dedicated to the idea that we all need some level of insurance protection to safeguard what little we have. We can purchase the coverage in a way which allows us to take advantage of the sound traditional principles which are the foundation of basic insurance protection. My website at www.christianmoney.com offers information and links for homeowners, life, health, and auto insurance.

TAKING ACTION
You can't afford not to have insurance.

If you don't have a lot of money, insurance protection is probably going to receive short shift in your budgeting. The problem with that is that your exposure to risk does not diminish as your bank account decreases in size. If you drive, you still run the risk of getting into an automobile accident; if you own a home, you still run the risks assumed by all homeowners, including fire, theft, and a plethora of other perils. The simple act of living exposes you to risks associated with your life and health, so you need to be covered for those as well. In short, although the purchase of insurance doesn't provide the same immediate gratification as does the purchase of food or the payment of your mortgage, you still need to place insurance protection near the top of your list of budgetary priorities. Insurance is a great example of something that takes more of your money in the short term in order to ensure that you don't have to pay out a lot more (or even declare bankruptcy) if you incur one of the risks covered by the insurance.

TAKING ACTION
Do not try to insure yourself against everything.

As important as insurance is, there's a right way and a wrong way to go about purchasing it. The first step to making sure that you pay as little as possible for your insurance protection is to be sure that you haven't purchased coverages which protect you against every conceivable risk. One of the slick marketing tools employed by the insurance industry has traditionally been to point out a risk which exists and then design a specific coverage for it. There are going to be risks everywhere you go, and it's going to be impossible to insure all of your risks unless you have millions of dollars earmarked to buy insurance. Did you know, for example, that it's possible to buy insurance that pays if you are mugged? (Granted, it would be nice to have insurance protection if that ever happens, but are you really in the position to pay for such coverage?)

The truth is, there are many examples of nonessential coverages out there, but if you are hard up for money you're not going to want to buy any of them. (I don't think you should buy any of them even if you aren't hard up for money!) You need to concentrate on covering the risks which are reasonable for your lifestyle. If you drive, you need auto insurance. If you own a home or rent a residence, you should have homeowners or renters insurance. You should also absolutely have health insurance. Finally, if you have dependents, life insurance is a must. If you have all of these coverages, you have the basic level of insurance protection against adverse financial risks you assume as a typical, everyday American.

One more thing. Beyond life, health, auto, and homeowners/renters insurance, some people cite the prudence of purchasing disability insurance as well. Many of these people point to statistics which show that for the bulk of your working life, the chances of suffering a disabling injury or illness are greater than the chances of dying. When you look at the situation in those terms, it makes sense to have disability coverage, doesn't it? Not so fast. Disability is one of those "iffy" kinds of policies which theoretically have some merit, but in practice are not all that prudent. We'll talk about disability coverage in depth a bit later (pp. 102-04).

TAKING ACTION

Self-insure as much as possible.

Whenever we talk about insurance, we're talking about the *risk* of something bad happening—not the certainty. This is the main reason why insurance protection does not always receive the priority it should in the family budget. After all, which makes more sense: Allocating money for the utility bill you know you will have, or allocating money for the insurance bill to indemnify you against a peril you *might* experience? Unfortunately, the basic risks associated with living your day-to-day existence are significant enough that you should protect them to some extent. This means, of course, that the purchase of insurance is not really an either/or proposition. You must find a way to cover both your ongoing expenses and insure against the calamities which could totally destroy your family's finances.

One of the best and easiest ways to keep the cost of your insurance down is to self-insure as much as possible. By self-insure I mean that you build up an insurance fund of your own that you can draw on in the event of an emergency. By self-insuring, you may not be able to completely forego the main types of coverages you should have, but you can limit the amount of each you'll need to purchase. We'll refer to the concept of self-insurance from time to time in the remainder of this chapter.

Life Insurance

TAKING ACTION

Only buy life insurance on wage-earners.

If you listen to some life insurance salespeople, you'll probably end up purchasing policies to cover every living thing in your household, including your dog and cat. There's always "a good reason" to have coverage on every member of your family. A key step to ensuring that you don't pay too much for life insurance is to make sure you're only covering those who *should* be covered. Let me explain.

The purpose of insurance is to fill an economic need. If your car is wrecked, you have auto insurance to pay for the damage. If your home is wrecked, you have homeowners insurance to pay for the losses. You have life insurance, then, to cover the losses incurred when a member of your family dies. Does this mean *any* member of your family? No! This only applies to those members who were covering the economic needs of the family. Certainly the primary breadwinner should be covered by life insurance. That's a given. If that person were to die, there's little chance that the family could survive financially without the replacement of his income or severe cutbacks. What about a wage-earner whose income is significant but not essential to the survival of the household? In that case, it becomes a judgment call on the part of the decision-makers in the family.

What about children? Should you have life insurance coverage on your children? The answer is basically no. I say *basically* because, although it's rare that children are ever in the position to provide for family subsistence, some people have found it prudent to purchase a small burial policy on kids in the event they meet an untimely death. In general, however, you want to stay away from insurance policies for children. (If you do insure your kids, never purchase a policy on a child for anything above $10,000.)

Keep in mind that if your family is structured so that one spouse works outside the home while the other is a homemaker, there is clear economic value associated with the role of homemaking. For example, if a full-time wife and mother were to die, the costs associated with childcare and homemaking would have to be covered. Now, this might not be possible right now due to budget concerns, but it's something to keep in mind when you gain more flexibility in your spending.

For now, make sure that only the significant wage-earners are covered. Once your new course of financial planning appears set, you can consider covering a full-time homemaker and *perhaps* children with policies appropriate to the situation. Consider canceling any current life insurance policies right away if they are not on essential wage-earners.

TAKING ACTION
Buy life insurance in the right amounts.

We know that life insurance is important, and it's important to insure only family wage-earners so that you don't waste your money. It's also important to make certain that you don't waste your money by insuring for more than necessary. It's not uncommon, for example, to see families insure the primary breadwinner for up to $1 million or even more. Certainly $1 million would be a big help in the event an important wage-earner and loved one passes away, but is it really necessary to pay for that much coverage for an event which is not expected and obviously discouraged? You need to be sure you're as adequately covered as possible *without* busting your budget.

The ideal rule of thumb when deciding how much insurance to purchase is an amount that if invested at 8 to 10% per year would yield a sum comparable to the annual salary lost by the death of the insured. For example, if a proposed insured earns $30,000 per year, he should probably be insured by a policy with a face amount somewhere between $300,000 to $375,000. Check the amounts for which the insureds in your family are currently covered. If they greatly exceed the amounts indicated by this rule, my suggestion is to lower the amount of the coverage as soon as possible and put the premium savings back in your pocket.

For those of you concerned that you can't pay for the amount of coverage suggested by the rule, remember that the rule of thumb is considered ideal. I'm *not* saying that if you can't afford to purchase insurance in accordance with this rule you should buy none at all. Every dollar of benefit will help you, so purchase what you can. Even if you can only afford a $50,000 policy, remember that's a $50,000 benefit to you and your family you otherwise would not have. A benefit lower than that recommended should buy you some time to help put your life back together and decide where to go from there.

TAKING ACTION
Only buy term insurance.

There are many different types of life insurance policies available for you to purchase, but in general they can be divided into two categories: whole life and term. Whole life insurance (also known as *cash value* life insurance) is designed to cover you for your *whole* life (hence the name). It is also set up to double as an investment where your premiums go, in part, to building up a cash accumulation account from which you can borrow later on. Another feature of whole life is the interest the policy earns. The biggest problem with whole life for cost-conscious, smart shoppers is that the combination of the guaranteed lifelong protection with the internal investment feature can make for exorbitant premiums. These so-called benefits which are rolled into this type of life insurance policy are made available because whole life overcharges you on your premiums during your younger years. Cash value is really an accumulated portion of the premiums you've paid through the years (which, by the way, the insurance company itself invests for a solid rate of return). Additionally, the interest earned by the policy is not all that helpful because it's added to the cash-value account—an account from which you may only borrow. If you owe money to your cash-value account when you die, the outstanding amount is withheld from the death benefit paid to your beneficiaries. There's one other thing you should know about cash-value insurance: The commissions paid to the salespeople of these policies are roughly ten times greater than those paid to salespeople of term life insurance. What does that tell you?

Term life insurance is such a great value because it doesn't pretend to be anything but pure life insurance. Again, what is the purpose of life insurance? To pay off sufficiently in the event of the death of a wage-earner, nothing more—no cash value, no interest, and so forth. Those other features were created by the insurance industry to turn life insurance into an enormous profit center. Whole life insurance premiums can cost you thousands of dollars a year for many, many years; a term life insurance policy with a face value of $250,000 can cost a 30-year-old nonsmoker as little as a few hundred dollars a year. Even $100,000 of term insurance can cost some folks as little as $10 per month! For people who are trying to find as many ways as possible to relieve the strain on their family budgets—but also recognize the importance of having life insurance—there's no contest. Term life insurance is the way to go.

If you currently have whole life insurance, you may want to consider getting rid of it in favor of term, especially if you're still at the point where your premiums are costing you an arm and a leg. However, remember: *Never drop important insurance coverages before you have purchased policies to replace them.* More than a few people have victimized themselves and their loved ones by dropping insurance policies before they had purchased replacement policies, only to find themselves befallen by catastrophe in the interim. It's better to continue paying for overpriced insurance in order to maintain coverage until you purchase new, less expensive coverage.

TAKING ACTION

Do not purchase term life until you've accessed a term-life policy search service.

Now that there is greater access to financial data that were formerly considered "insider information" many different services and programs have been developed to help consumers save money on their purchases of financial products. One of the very best new services is the lowest-cost insurance policy search service. There are many organizations now in existence that search for the nation's term insurers that offer the lowest-cost policy for consumers. Check out the "Term Life Shopper" link at www.christianmoney.com.

Health Insurance

TAKING ACTION

Use major medical coverage for protection against serious illness or accidents.

There's a lot of confusion regarding health insurance. People who have been exposed at one time or another to comprehensive group health insurance seem to believe that there is only one type of health insurance—the kind with all the "bells and whistles."

You know what I'm talking about . . . the $15 doctor visits, the $5 prescriptions, and so on. Because those kinds of coverages are made available to a group where the expense of the plan is spread out over a large number of people, the per-person cost of the coverage is usually pretty reasonable. Therein lies part of the problem. If you have ever had that kind of coverage, it's tough to forget. If you no longer have it available through a group, or never had it to begin with, you *can* purchase such a policy on an individual basis—but it's unbelievably expensive. If you currently maintain an individually purchased, comprehensive health-insurance plan that could easily be part of why your budget is at its breaking point. Unless you have family members who are so chronically ill that it's cheaper for you to continue paying for the expensive policy, you might want to consider another alternative: major medical, also known as hospitalization.

With major medical, you receive only the most basic coverage. You don't receive the dirt-cheap office visits or prescriptions, but you do have a policy which will pay if you or a family member is involved in a serious accident or hit with an illness that requires hospitalization. In fact, major medical is becoming such a popular option that many insurers are finding themselves in competition for this market. This means that some companies are beginning to offer more benefits as part of their major medical coverage than others. Whatever you do, don't make the mistake of assuming that medical catastrophes won't touch you or a member of your family. If you have no coverage whatsoever and something happens, your family could easily be driven into bankruptcy. Even a relatively minor operation like the removal of an appendix can leave you with medical bills in the thousands. Think of everything you do each day, from driving a car, to playing sports, to "horseplaying" around the house with family members that could potentially result in an accident requiring hospitalization. As far as illnesses go, we all know there are many kinds of germs and viruses around. Who's to say that you'll never contract any disease of any kind during your lifetime? Do not assume that you can afford to walk around unprotected—you can't.

TAKING ACTION

To make major medical policies even more affordable, keep the deductible high.

The deductible of any insurance policy is the amount you pay before the insurance company starts to pay. As you can probably guess, the lower your deductible, the more expensive your premiums because you're asking the insurance company to pay more. The key is to keep the deductible as high as possible without losing the value of having insurance in the first place. You could, for instance, keep your deductible at $5,000, which means that the cost of your monthly premiums would be very low, which is good. The problem is whether you have the $5,000 to pay toward medical bills in the event of an accident or illness. Since this isn't likely, your goal is to keep the deductible high, but not so high that the value of having insurance is greatly reduced. A common deductible settled on by folks in this predicament is $1,000. They're willing to pay the first $1,000 of injury or illness in an effort to keep the cost of the insurance premiums down. Because many hospitalizations and in-patient services can easily cost well into the thousands, they feel they're still receiving a good value in maintaining their health coverage.

TAKING ACTION

To lower your cost even further, purchase a policy with a copayment provision.

By deciding to purchase a major-medical policy with a high deductible, you have probably done about as much as you can to provide medical coverage for yourself and your family at as low a rate as possible. There is, however, a little more you can do with the structure of the policy. Agree to a copayment provision within the policy.

Having a copayment provision within an insurance policy means that you agree to chip in for the costs faced by the insurance company in paying your bills. For example, a common rate of copayment is "80–20," which means that after the deductible is paid, you and the insurance company agree to split the remainder of the bill. The insurer pays for 80% of the amount above the deductible; you pay for the remainder. Agreeing to a copayment provision can significantly reduce the amount of your premium because, like the high deductible, you are assuming a greater portion of the financial risk.

Many people offhandedly balk at the notion of agreeing to a copayment provision, stating that between the copayment and the high deductible, they might as well skip the cost of health insurance altogether. Big mistake. Let's look at this in terms of real numbers. If you incur a $10,000 medical bill under the terms of a $1,000 deductible and an 80–20 copayment provision, you are out-of-pocket $3,800. Certainly $3,800 is not an insignificant sum of money, but no one can argue that it's not considerably less than $10,000, which is what you *would* have had to pay if you had no insurance at all.

Remember, too, that the kind of copayment provision you elect should represent a good balance between low cost and policy value. A very common copayment provision is one which caps at $5,000. This means that in the case of the 80–20 copay with the $1,000 deductible, you would have to pay the first $1,000 of your bill, you and the insurance company would split the rest of the bill up to $5,000 (80–20), and then the insurance company would pay for everything above the $5,000 mark. This is a good way for you to realize some of the available benefit of opting for a copayment provision without running the risk of paying thousands upon thousands of dollars in the event of a major medical crisis in your family.

TAKING ACTION

Avail yourself of computerized search services to find the best deals in major-medical coverage.

The best way to get a good deal for insurance purchases is to shop around. That probably sounds like no-brainer advice to you, but you may not realize how significant the savings can be. For reasons which may appear obvious, auto insurance generally offers the greatest disparity in rates, but *all* types of insurance are prone to great differences among carriers. Health insurance is no different. To help ensure that you're getting the best deal possible, I recommend that you shop through a computerized clearing house of companies before you make a decision. There are several companies out there that do this kind of service. Go to www.christianmoney.com for helpful links to getting medical insurance quotes.

Disability Insurance

TAKING ACTION

Weigh your decision to purchase disability
insurance very carefully.

Disability insurance is one of those insurance purchases that I consider to be "on the line." By that I mean I'm not always convinced that it's a waste of money to have it, but at the same time there's a lot wrong with how it works currently. You have to put a lot of thought into the prospective purchase of this type of coverage. Let me show you what I mean.

Statistics will tell you that you are more likely to become disabled during your working years than you are to die. That would seem to make the case for disability coverage, right? After all, if you're going to buy life insurance, then it surely makes sense to purchase coverage for a risk which is greater than one you're already buying for.

Although the idea behind disability insurance is excellent (that you would be paid if you became disabled and couldn't work), the insurance industry has twisted and turned the coverage into such a configuration that it's barely recognizable. First of all, disability coverage is expensive. As if that alone weren't bad enough, the industry has developed very tough standards as to what qualifies as a disability—and the policy will only pay if you meet *those* standards.

There are two basic types of disability insurance. One is called "your occupation," and the other is called "any occupation." "Your occupation" coverage pays in the event you are disabled to the point where you can no longer work in your particular career. "Any occupation" coverage will pay if you are disabled to the point where you cannot perform in *any* career. Now, ask yourself: "How likely is it that I will become disabled to the point that I will not be able to work again?" Probably not very. Insurance companies do not like to pay claims, and you can be certain that they will work awfully hard to avoid having to pay on the claim by finding something else you can do in your condition. Ask yourself another question: "How likely is it that I will ever become disabled to the point that I can no longer perform in my chosen career?" That's probably going to take a little more thought on your part. Remember, though, that you will have to satisfy the insurance company as to the extent of your disability before you see a dime of claim money.

If you're carrying disability insurance now and are having a hard time making ends meet, ask yourself why you've got it and if it's the wisest expenditure of your money at this time. I'm not going to tell you to drop it because, with my luck, you'll do so and have a disabling accident next week. You should, however, think long and hard about the prudence of spending money on disability insurance with respect to your current lifestyle.

TAKING ACTION

If you keep or purchase disability coverage, select a long elimination period.

The *elimination period* of a disability insurance policy is that amount of time you must be disabled before you can begin collecting. The shorter the elimination period, the more the insurance company has to pay and, consequently, the more you'll pay in premiums. The longer the period, the less the insurance company has to pay, so the less you have to pay for coverage. If you decide that it's not a waste of money to have a disability policy, you can keep your costs down by requesting a fairly long elimination period—perhaps between six months and a year. This means you will have to cover the expenses incurred during the elimination period out of your own pocket—but it does keep costs down.

TAKING ACTION
Build your own disability policy.

The decision whether to purchase insurance is a constant battle between the cost of coverage and the likelihood of collecting. Although statistics tell us that you're more likely to become disabled than you are to die (at least in your younger years), the insurance industry has made it difficult for you to collect on a disability policy. A good answer for someone who would like to be covered for a disabling accident or illness, but also would like to save money, is to have that person set up his own disability fund. Rather than pay premiums for years and then have to pay the expenses during a long elimination period, you might decide that you would be better off setting aside about six months' worth of living expenses in a fund earmarked to draw from if you suffer a disabling injury or illness. This fund could be the basic cash reserve we spoke about in the chapter "Financial Freedom on a Budget," or it could be a fund designated exclusively for disability. Either way, funding your own disability policy is a good way to give yourself some protection against a disabling event *without* having to play risky money games with the insurance company.

Auto Insurance

TAKING ACTION

Do not try to get by without auto insurance.

Whenever rules or principles to save money are outlined, it's prudent to include some that dictate spending *some* money in the short term to protect your larger financial interests in the long term. This notion pertains most obviously to the area of insurance, where many people are prone to turn a blind eye to the potential financial risks which face them on a daily basis. It's amazing how many people continue to walk through life believing that misfortunes only afflict "the other guy." It never dawns on most people who ascribe to this philosophy that, to everyone else out there, *they* are the other guy. The vast majority of us *do need* to purchase some kind of financial protection against the many risks which are hiding out there, waiting to trip us up.

If you drive an automobile, you should have auto insurance. Fortunately, most states require all drivers to have insurance. They have stringent laws to punish people who dare to drive without it. Some people continue to do so, tempting fate every time they get behind the wheel. I know that auto insurance can represent quite a drain on a budget each month, but owning a car is a substantial enough risk to warrant paying for solid coverage. If you don't have coverage of any kind at this moment, you need to get some. The problem with trying to get by without automobile insurance is that, by its very nature, driving a car is dangerous business. As greater numbers of people take to the roads at all hours of the day and night, your chances of becoming involved in a mishap rise significantly. This is to say nothing of the risks you take by just owning an automobile. Weather-related difficulties and natural disasters have been known to destroy their share of autos, and auto theft is still on the rise throughout America. Yes, if you want to drive a car in this day and age, it is more important than ever that you maintain some measure of automobile coverage.

Note that I said "some measure." If you're having a tough time getting your budget to balance each month, one of the first places to look for relief is your auto policy. This *doesn't* mean you should drop your auto policy. It means you should maintain a smartly purchased one. Automobile insurance can be had and can be affordable for most people, but it helps to check out the options before you go out to buy it.

TAKING ACTION
The most important element to finding affordable auto insurance is shopping around.

When asked how to get the best deal on a financial product or service, financial experts often respond with "you must shop around." How many times have you heard *that!* Gee, is that what counts as expert advice today? My response to those sarcastic barbs is that if the advice is such a no-brainer, then how come you still see such a disparity in rates among insurers?

Even though most people consider the recommendation to shop around obvious, in practice most of us don't do it like we should. As a result, many insurance companies can feel confident charging rates which sit at the high end of the scale because they know that most people will not check out prices. Insurance companies will still get their share of customers. Shopping around doesn't mean simply trying two or three insurers; it means assembling a list that's at least five or six companies deep and getting a definable quote from each one. Ideally, you want to take the time and effort to get a quote from as many companies as humanly possible. Sound excessive? Let me tell you something: On the subject of auto insurance, it is not unheard of to find quotes for the same coverage made to a given family that vary by as much as $1,000 among insurers. *That's $1,000 per year variance for the same coverage!* This means that these families for whom this kind of disparity exists could potentially pay as much as $83 per month *more* for coverage than they would otherwise have to pay. How much are *you* paying for auto insurance coverage? Are you getting a good deal? How do you know? To effectively shop, however, you need to know what kind of specific coverages and deductibles you want within your auto policy. We'll talk more about that in just a bit.

Before we move on, however, it's important to me that you have as much motivation as possible to shop your policy out. To that end, I've included a checklist form to help you begin your search (p. 109). Read the rest of this section before you begin to look around, but make certain that you *do* begin to look around soon. If you're suffering from not having enough money at the end of the month, you may find a lot of help from the simple act of shopping out your auto policy.

To give you a further head start on your mission, I've included a short list of auto insurance companies which various consumer publications have found to offer some of the better deals in recent years. My recommendation would be to put these companies at the top of your checklist. Begin your search!

USAA
800-531-8319

Erie Insurance Exchange
800-458-0811

Geico
800-841-3000

Liberty Mutual
(Consult Yellow Pages for local office)

Progressive
800-288-6776

Nationwide Mutual
(Consult Yellow Pages for local office)

TAKING ACTION

Keep your auto policy deductible high.

Many people who purchase automobile insurance aren't aware that they have a choice when it comes to the amount of the deductible they want to carry. They believe that a $250 deductible is as natural and as appropriate as getting up in the morning and having breakfast. Well, if it is, it's only because the industry isn't going out of its way to inform you otherwise. Remember when Burger King's slogan said that you could "have it your way"? Well, you *can* have it your way when it comes to auto insurance as well, particularly when it comes to selecting a deductible. If you are carrying a deductible of $100 currently, you're paying way too much for auto insurance. It's as simple as

Auto Insurance Checklist

Insurance Company	Telephone	Agent	Date

Quotes/Notes

Quotes/Notes

Quotes/Notes

Quotes/Notes

Quotes/Notes

Quotes/Notes

that—and no amount of shopping around is going to help if you insist on keeping the deductible that low.

Remember when we spoke about the concept of "self-insurance"—when you save money in a special fund? Consider doing that here as well. Insure yourself for as much as the first $1,000 of a mishap, and you'll see the cost of your auto premiums plummet. If a $1,000 deductible seems a little steep, what about $500? The point is that raising your deductible will save you as much as 25% of the cost of your policy for each incremental hike of $250.

There's another advantage to raising your deductible that should be mentioned even though it doesn't relate as directly to the issue of cost. If you keep your deductible low, say at the $250 or $100 level, you'll be tempted to make a claim every time you suffer a loss beyond those dollar levels. And every time you have a claim your insurance company raises your rates. Worse still, after too many claims, your insurer will cancel your policy altogether, leaving you stranded. Play it safe and deprive yourself of the motivation to run to the insurance company with low-dollar claims by self-insuring for the first $500 to $1,000 of losses.

TAKING ACTION

Drop collision coverage
if your car falls below $2,000 in value.

Collision can be a very expensive part of your automobile policy, chiefly because it's one of the main reasons you purchase auto insurance to begin with. Collision coverage reimburses you in the event your car is damaged in an accident. The coverage is typically made mandatory by the lender when you buy a new car on credit, so that their interests are protected. Even if you paid cash for the car, you want to keep collision coverage on the vehicle— even a few minor scratches can cost you a couple hundred dollars in your efforts to bring the car back to pristine condition. Imagine what your out-of-pocket expenses would be if you had to pay to repair your vehicle after a sizable accident! Collision is an essential part of your auto coverage and one well worth paying for…up to a point.

The problem with collision coverage is that after some years it becomes cost-ineffective to maintain. To understand this, you have to be aware that an insurer will never give you more than the car is worth. This means that if your once-new vehicle is now worth $2,000, the insurer will not pay you $3,000 to repair it after an accident. All you'll receive is the $2,000. Now you may be thinking, *Hey, if it costs $3,000 to fix and I want it fixed, then they should pay.* That's not how it works. Despite your maintenance of collision coverage, the insurer is not obligated to give you more to fix the vehicle than it's worth. And he won't. This is why many financial planners recommend dropping collision coverage when the value of the car falls somewhere between $1,500 and $2,000. Collision coverage is very expensive, and its price does not drop as the value of your vehicle recedes. Does this mean that you are responsible to pay needed repair costs out of your own pocket in the event of an accident? Yes, indeed. However, assuming you're not so attached to the car that you'd be willing to pay over its value to fix it, that's probably a fair gamble to take in order to save some significant money in the cost of your auto policy. A lot of you are probably driving automobiles that are at least a few years old, and some may be a lot older. Think seriously about dropping your collision coverage if your car has fallen below the $2,000 mark—or at least take steps to self-insure for the $2,000 (which can either go toward repair bills or the cost of a new car!).

TAKING ACTION
Drop comprehensive coverage if your car falls below $2,000 in value.

The purpose of comprehensive coverage is to reimburse you for the costs of fixing your car when it is damaged during circumstances other than a collision. For example, if the car is damaged by weather or if it is damaged during the course of a theft attempt, comprehensive will pay for the repair costs. Again, we face the same issues with comprehensive coverage as we do with collision: Policy cost versus benefit realized. If the car is only worth $1,000 to $2,000 at this point, there's really little point in maintaining an expensive part of your auto coverage which will pay you relatively little. Remember, too, that if you raise your deductible to $500 or even $1,000, the value of having comprehensive (and your collision, too) is lessened because you're already agreeing to pay for the first $500 to $1,000 worth of damage—no matter what.

TAKING ACTION
Drop frivolous coverages in your auto policy.

Most auto policies give you the option of purchasing various types of what I call frivolous coverages, such as towing privileges and roadside assistance. These perks are nice to have if you can afford them. If you're having a tough time making ends meet right now, you should drop them as soon as you can. In truth, these perk coverages are not terribly expensive (unless you have a lot of them), but if you're currently in the position where every dollar matters, I wouldn't waste any more money on them. Get your auto policy and closely examine it to see if you're carrying any of these extras. If so, call your agent and ask that they be dropped immediately.

TAKING ACTION

Drop medical payments coverage as long as you have health insurance in force.

One of the big no-nos when buying insurance of any type is to pay for duplicate coverages. If you haven't scrutinized your auto policy with a discerning consumer's eye before this, it's very likely that you're carrying something called "medical payments" coverage as part of your policy. In a nutshell, medical payments coverage is health insurance which covers you in the event you suffer an auto-related accident. This is not a bad piece of protection to have unless you already have health insurance (which you should!). If you do, drop your medical payments coverage as soon as you can.

Homeowners Insurance

Stick to HO-1 coverage
when buying your homeowners policy.

There are six different kinds of homeowners insurance policies in existence. If you're having a difficult time managing your finances right now, you should consider maintaining only the most basic kind of homeowners insurance coverage. If your home is more recently built, this means having HO-1. If it is older, you may need HO-8. These policies cover you for the basics, including fire, theft, smoke damage, vandalism, hail—the usual stuff. HO-2 policies go further, covering you if your house is damaged by such things as the weight of ice or snow, frozen plumbing, and the accidental cracking or tearing of a heater or air conditioner. HO-3 policies are even more comprehensive (and more expensive), covering you for everything except those perils which are specifically mentioned as being excluded from coverage. If you're in a financial bind, make certain that you're covered for no more than the basics. Anything else is a waste of premium.

Keep your homeowners
deductible high.

Here we go again with the deductible discussion, but it's as relevant here as it is with any other type of insurance policy. The deductible is your contribution to the coverage of the loss. If the insurance company is on the hook for less, then your policy will cost you less. I suggest keeping your homeowners deductible at somewhere between the $500 and $1,000 mark. Keeping the deductible relatively high will help you out on the cost of your policy, and, as is the case with auto insurance, it will keep you from making too many claims, which may result in an increase in your premiums or even cancellation of your policy.

TAKING ACTION
Insist that your policy covers only the structure, not the land.

In general, homeowners policies are set up in such a fashion that 80% of the policy's value is ascribed to the structure, while the remaining 20% is earmarked to cover the land. Under what circumstances will your land ever become unusable? I suppose it's possible in the most unlikely of circumstances, but you're not in the position to cover unlikely circumstances. You can only afford to cover the basics. Call your agent and insist that your policy be issued or reissued so that it covers the actual dwelling only and not the land on which it sits.

TAKING ACTION
Be certain that your home is insured for at least 80% of replacement costs.

This is one of those "caveat principles"—one which asks you to spend a little more money in order to get a lot more protection.

Throughout this entire discussion of insurance, we must always be mindful of the risks of purchasing too little coverage. This subject is relevant to homeowners insurance as well. In this case, you want to make sure you purchase homeowners which provides for a minimum of 80% of the replacement cost of your home. Replacement cost for 100% is really what you're after, but if you find that to be too expensive, consider 80%. Dropping to 80% will cut your premiums significantly, but will not expose you to so great a risk that it seriously weakens the point of having homeowner's in the first place.

Let's talk for a moment about why having replacement coverage within a homeowners policy is so important. If you don't have replacement coverage, you will be reimbursed only for the value of the article at the time of loss. This means that a stereo which cost $1,500 new several years ago and is destroyed in a fire may only be worth a few hundred dollars now. What you *want* is enough money to go out and *replace* that stereo. Replacement coverage will do that for you. Replacement coverage *is* more expensive (it raises your premiums about 15 to 25% higher than what they would be otherwise). It's definitely worth paying for if you want real protection and the means to recover financially if you suffer a significant loss.

Become an Investor
for $50 a Month!

D o you wonder why I've included a chapter on investing in this book? After all, it takes a lot of money to invest in stocks, bonds, mutual funds, and other securities, right? The truth is, it doesn't. Investing is a highly misunderstood endeavor, based in large part on the assumption that it takes a huge amount of money to do it. There was a time when it was tough to invest your money unless you had a fair amount to begin with, but the investment world has changed in some significant ways. Now, access by people without great sums of money is quite viable.

Are you wondering if you should start investing even though you're still in debt? My answer may surprise you! First, let me say that the principal reason most people have debt is that they don't have any savings. Therefore, breaking the cycle of indebtedness is more important than just paying off one's current debts. In other words, let's first extinguish the reason that you have debt and then work on paying off your debts altogether. In order to do this, I suggest that a balanced approach be employed. The balance I recommend is to invest half of your monthly surplus and use the other half for debt reduction. By following this simple formula you will eventually become debt free. You'll also be building your own reserve account which will eliminate the need to use debt in the future! Let's look at investment possibilities.

Perhaps the greatest advance in the realm of low-cost investing has been the mutual fund. The mutual fund, by its very structure, makes investing a better prospect for those with little money. Mutual funds, rather than being individual stocks themselves, are investment companies whose business is to *invest* in individual stocks. Right off the bat, this makes investing in stocks much more cost-effective because the mutual fund manager takes the sums invested in his fund and uses it to buy a portfolio of securities. If you have only $500 to invest, for example, you probably have avoided investing in individual stocks. Stocks of popular companies usually have a pretty substantial share price, which means you would not have been able to purchase many shares. Furthermore, if you buy your stocks through a full-service brokerage (the well-known Merrill Lynch and Paine Webber are examples of two such companies), you will spend a significant portion of that $500 simply on the broker's commission. With a mutual fund, however, your $500 would go into a pool with the money invested by many other folks. That money, collectively, is used to purchase stocks of individual companies. It's like the mutual fund is one giant investor with a whole bunch of money to invest. However, the mutual fund is a security itself, which means that when you invest your $500, your investment buys shares of the fund. The price of these shares is dependent largely on the prices of the underlying stocks. It's a little complicated, but now you have the gist of mutual fund investing.

"That's great," you might say, "but I haven't got $500 to invest," or "Hey, I bought this book because I've got next to nothing!" Fair enough. Again, enter the mutual fund to save the day. Because the mutual fund industry has grown by leaps and bounds over the course of the last 20 years, there are now ways you can invest for less than $500…much, much less. We'll talk about them later in this chapter.

Mutual funds are perhaps the best way for inexperienced investors to invest small amounts of money in securities, but there are others. The point is, you have to have an open mind. You cannot assume at the outset of our discussion that there is no way to invest small sums of money. There is. Granted, doing so may not be as exciting as investing a lot of money. And you don't get the opportunity to realize the kind of return in raw dollars that others do. The "feel" of investing may not be the same if you're just putting in a little bit at a time. However, make no mistake about it: You are investing. What you start building up today may turn into a substantial portfolio over the course of your life. The key is to stay motivated and to keep from getting discouraged by what you may perceive to be a slow growth of your money.

TAKING ACTION

Realize your long-term goals and dreams via no-load mutual funds.

We have touched briefly on mutual funds, talking chiefly about how their structure makes them conducive to investment by folks with very little money. That's true. However, did you know that some mutual funds have an additional feature which makes them even more advantageous to the person with little money? It's true. It's known as being "no-load."

In the investment community, the word "load" is synonymous with the word "commission." Commissions, as you are probably aware, are the fees a company pays to its salespeople for selling its products. Many mutual funds are designed to be sold through agents and brokers, and thus they carry commissions of anywhere from 4 to 8%. It's important that you don't miss the significance of this. If you invest $100 in a mutual fund which carries, say, a 5% commission, only $95 of your $100 actually goes to purchase shares of the fund. The other $5 goes into the salesperson's pocket. That may not sound like a lot at first—until you learn that it's completely unnecessary. There are a great number of excellent mutual funds out there which don't assess loads of any kind, which means that all of the money you invest goes right to work for you by buying fund shares. These kinds of funds are referred to as "no-load" mutual funds.

If you don't have much money to work with, one of your first priorities when it comes to investing should be to cut out the middleman (the broker, in this case) as much as possible. With mutual funds, you can do that entirely. At any given time, you'll find that any list of the top-performing mutual funds is comprised as much by no-load funds as by load funds. You don't have to sacrifice quality or performance in order to save some money. When it comes to funds, you can indeed have it all.

One of the more common questions posed by people who first learn about the differences between load and no-load funds is, "How do no-load funds make their money if they don't charge a commission?" The answer to that question lies in your understanding about the mechanics of mutual funds. All mutual funds, it should be noted, charge management fees of between 1 and 2%. The purpose of these fees is to compensate the actual fund manager, his team of analysts, and pay other costs associated with operating the fund. Note that I said *all* funds, both load and no-load, charge these fees. The commission charged by load funds is assessed in addition to this management fee, and its sole purpose is to compensate the brokers who sell them. No-load funds do not charge commissions because they do not use brokers in the field to sell them; no-load fund companies chiefly use mainstream media outlets to market their funds directly to the public. When you purchase your no-load fund, you do it through the mail by filling out the application the fund company sends you and returning it, along with a check for the amount of your investment. Once your application and check are processed, you'll receive a confirmation of your purchase in the mail. Your career as an investor has officially begun.

While I have never been a big fan of load funds for the reasons I've just outlined, I must confess that some people just seem more comfortable when they've paid a commission. For example, one of the reasons some people suggest for choosing loads over no-loads is that when you purchase a load fund from a broker, you've now availed yourself of the right to contact that broker and receive guidance on your investment strategy and your portfolio as a whole. No-load fund customer service representatives, who are usually the only people you'll ever speak to at their company, cannot offer that kind of advice. While you'll find that, indeed, no-load fund reps will not be able to give you any guidance as to investment strategies, be aware of the fact that the "benefit" of being able to talk to your broker when you buy a load fund is not usually all it's cracked up to be. In my experience in the investment industry, I've noticed that while the purchaser of a load fund should be able to access his broker whenever he needs to, most brokers don't really want to talk to a client unless he's interested in buying more shares of the fund or another investment product. As soon as your broker gets the message that you're not calling to buy anything else which will pay him a commission, he will probably have his secretary or someone else deflect your calls until you become exasperated and stop calling. This will be especially true with respect to a client who doesn't have much money to begin with because he or she isn't responsible for the broker receiving a very big payday.

To circumvent all of this, stick to no-load mutual funds. You'll find that these are, overall, the best gifts ever given to the small investor.

TAKING ACTION

How not having much to invest can force you to be the smartest of investors.

Let me guess. You think having little to invest puts you at a serious disadvantage to making money. Well, I know what you're getting at, but I have some news which will undoubtedly surprise you. If you have only a little bit of money to place into an investment each month, you will, by that very "limitation," be required to follow one of the smartest, most time-honored strategies of investment success ever devised: Dollar cost averaging.

Dollar cost averaging works like this: Instead of depositing a sizable lump sum of money into a mutual fund, the investor opts to invest his or her money in smaller sums over a long period of time on a regular basis (like monthly). The idea is to limit one's exposure to market risk by not committing the money all at once, to be guided in its entirety by the forces of the market. Let's say, for example, that you have $2,000 to invest in mutual funds.

Your first inclination might be to dump it all in the fund(s) at once—but wait. What happens if the market as a whole reacts negatively to some unforeseen bad news and drops several hundred points shortly after you have placed your money? There's really nothing you can do because you've placed all the money. You now must wait for the market to begin an extended upward surge before you can begin to make any money.

When you invest in smaller sums over a longer period of time, however, you are largely mitigating that risk. Let's say you invest your $2,000 by doing it $100 at a time over the course of 20 months. When the shares of your selected fund are lower priced, the money buys more shares; when they're priced higher, your $100 buys fewer. The key is that you do not unnecessarily expose your money to the all-too-familiar uncertainty we've seen within the stock market.

Can you see, then, the advantage that having just a little money each month to invest gives you? By investing, say, $50 each month into a fund, you are automatically taking part in dollar cost averaging. Granted, you don't have much of a choice, but so what? If you *had* the $2,000 to invest, you might be too tempted to dump it all into the market at one time, thereby taking the wrong approach to your investing.

By the way, you might be thinking, "Hey, I can see the benefit of dollar cost averaging if we assume the market will go down right after I place my lump sum, but won't I lose out if I dollar cost average and it takes off immediately?" At first it might seem that way, but understand that proper investing is a long-term proposition. The market will go up and down continually (but moves upward more often), so you want to mitigate the effect of that negative short-term movement but maintain your market position nonetheless.

TAKING ACTION

Yes, there really are no-load mutual funds that will let you invest for $50 each month!

If you're like most people, you believe that investing is only for the rich—or at least for those people who have extra money. While you do need to have *some* money to invest, you might be surprised at how little you need in order to get started. There are a number of high-quality, no-load mutual funds out there which will waive their minimum lump-sum investment requirements if you agree to deposit as little as $100 per month into them (until you reach the minimum). "Wait a minute," you say. All right. One hundred dollars per month isn't bad, but you can't swing even that much. Okay, how about $50 per month? That's right, there are terrific funds out there that will let you get started for only $50 per month. What? $50 per month is still too much? If you find that things are so tight for you right now that you aren't able to muster even the $50 per month to get started, then you may want to open a savings account and start to set aside whatever you can…$10 per month, $5 per month, perhaps even less. When you get to the point where you have met at least the minimum for some funds by setting aside a little at a time, then you can invest.

There are lots of ways you can become a real investor. You should not let your money shortage stand in the way of reaching your goals and dreams. There's just no reason for it.

To help you get started, Appendix A lists no-load mutual fund families that accept $50 in monthly payments. There are also websites of a few funds you can check out. My website www.christianmoney.com also lists low-cost mutual funds and DRIP programs. (For more on DRIPs see pp. 129-31.)

Kill two birds with one stone:
Set up your retirement plan and invest for
lower minimums through an IRA.

If you're like most people who don't have very much money, a lot of important financial tools that have the potential to aid you greatly never seem to get purchased. Insurance is an example of one such tool that comes quickly to mind. Many people go without valuable coverages because they don't have the means to pay for them. (I talk about getting around this problem in the chapter "Protecting Your Family's Future Through Insurance.") Insurance is not the only example, although it may be the best. Another good financial tool that can offer great assistance to individuals but is often overlooked is a tax-deferred retirement plan. If your employer does not offer one, you must set one up on your own. Unfortunately, many people balk at doing so. They believe that there is a lot of paperwork involved and that they need to go into the plan with a chunk of money up front. The fact is, neither is true. You can set up an Individual Retirement Account (IRA) in a matter of minutes with any no-load mutual fund company. What's more, you can oftentimes set it up with a lower initial minimum investment than you would need if you were setting up a mutual fund as a fully-taxable account.

Think of your IRA as a box. Anything you put in the box grows tax deferred and may create a tax deduction for you as well. A mutual fund is one of myriad investment options you can choose to put in your "IRA box." Keep in mind that an IRA is not an investment in and of itself, but only a special account with tax advantages. Therefore what you put inside your IRA is as important as having an IRA in the first place.

If you look at an in-depth profile of a mutual fund company, you will usually see that the minimum initial investment requirements are much lower if you're opening the fund of your choice within an IRA or other tax-deferred retirement account. The beauty of this arrangement? Not only do you have a wider selection of fund companies and individual funds available to you, but setting up the account as an IRA is the first step toward realizing a successful retirement.

TAKING ACTION
Build a professional, diversified portfolio of mutual funds through a discount broker and pay no commissions.

It seems that very often it is folks who have the least who also have the grandest dreams. That's probably not so tough to understand, but it is these people who must work that much harder and find more unconventional ways to realize their dreams. When it comes to investing, many neophytes learn fast, and they become impatient to try to achieve their dreams as quickly as possible. If you don't have much money, however, it becomes much more difficult to play like the "big boys" . . . difficult, but not impossible. You just have to know where to look for the right opportunities.

If you want to become an investment guru or "player" with an honest-to-goodness portfolio of mutual funds but feel that such a portfolio is well beyond your financial grasp, then you're in for a surprise. Many discount brokerages, intent on grabbing a chunk of the no-load mutual fund customer base, have seen fit to set up programs that allow investors to buy and sell mutual funds through their companies for no commissions or transaction fees whatsoever. You might be thinking, *What's the big deal? I can already buy and sell these no-load mutual funds on my own through the fund companies.* That's true, but you can't do it like this.

If you own XYZ fund which you purchased through the XYZ Fund Company, but want to switch to another fund, you must first sell XYZ fund, receive your proceeds, and open an account at ABC Fund Company to buy ABC fund. Not only is such an arrangement administratively tedious, it prohibits trading funds on a timely basis. However, if you purchase your no-load funds through a discount broker you will be able to trade your XYZ fund for the ABC fund simply on the basis of a phone call. Furthermore, all the funds you own will be carried on a single monthly statement, adding clarity to your investing. (Charles Schwab & Co. [800-435-4000] is a good example of companies that offer discount broker services. You can also go to www.schwab.com.)

If you aspire to be a real investment player, juggling a lot of balls in the air, you can do it even if you don't have much money. Just give Charles Schwab & Co. (or another discount broker with a similar program) a call and tell them you want to get started.

TAKING ACTION
Avoid retail stock brokers.

If you don't have much experience with investing, the only names in the investment community you may be aware of are probably those like Merrill Lynch, Dean Witter, Prudential Bache, and the other Wall Street firms that advertise regularly on television. They also have long histories providing investment services and products to the public. While these may be the most famous companies in the investment community, they are the firms you should avoid if you are trying to invest on a limited budget. These firms are known as full-service retail firms, which means that they provide a number of services beyond those offered by discounters like Schwab. Some of those services can be quite helpful, including furnishing research reports on the various individual companies their customers may be considering for investment. The problem is that you will pay dearly for those services. The average commission on a stock trade made through a full-service retail operation is about 5%; it is much lower through the discounters. *Sure*, you may be thinking, *but those perks would be nice to have—and maybe they're worth paying the extra commission.*

While you might like having them, they're not necessary to your investment success—and anything that's not necessary you should not be buying. Besides, the added features are not always everything they seem to be. As I said earlier, one of the supposed advantages to buying a load mutual fund is the right to talk to your broker whenever you need advice. But the reality is that he (or she) won't want to spend much time speaking with you unless you're buying more product from him.

The same thing applies here. The 5% commission is supposed to entitle you to ongoing service from your broker, but I can tell you right now that once he realizes you don't have a lot of money to spend, he will do his best to avoid your calls.

Although it may mean doing more homework on your own, you and your wallet will be much better off if you stick to no-load mutual funds, discount brokers, and other low-cost ways of investing. In fact, let's discuss how to invest in individual stocks, long considered the most difficult vehicles to buy inexpensively, as cheaply as possible.

To invest in stocks as cheaply as possible, participate in dividend reinvestment plans.

We've seen how it's possible to invest in mutual funds very cheaply and for very little minimum investment. What if you want to purchase individual stocks? Is there any way to do that as inexpensively as you can purchase mutual funds? While it's not possible quite yet to purchase individual stocks completely commission-free, that day may not be too far in the future. In the meantime, there is a way to purchase stocks for next to no commission whatsoever. The mechanism which allows this is known as the dividend reinvestment plan (DRIP).

The dividend reinvestment plan allows current shareholders of a company to purchase additional shares of stock directly *from* the company, thereby sidestepping the broker and his commission. Not all publicly traded companies offer DRIPs, but many of the largest and best-known companies do. As the name suggests, the plan works by having the investor reinvest his dividend checks directly back into the company to buy more shares of stock. This plan wouldn't be suitable for an investor who needs his dividend checks for subsistence purposes or who otherwise has designs on spending the money. However, for a person who is looking for a cheap way to become a regular investor in specific, individual companies and wants growth over the long term, the DRIP is tough to beat.

For more information on DRIPs, check out my website at www.christianmoney.com and click on "No Load Stocks." This will take you to links that provide general investor advice, more information on DRIPs, and specifics on getting started in investing.

The only aspect to enrolling in a DRIP that the penny-pinching investor must contend with has to do with the initial purchase of stock. Remember, DRIPs are only available to *current* shareholders. This means that to get on board, you must have already purchased the requisite number of shares from a broker. At this point you may be thinking, *Uh-oh, I probably have to buy a thousand shares of a particular company to get started in its DRIP program.* Now, really, do you think I would have included the DRIP opportunity in this book if that were the case? While it's true that some companies require that you own 50 shares or so before you enroll, most will let you climb on board if you own just one share. In order to keep your costs down, you probably should consider purchasing your initial shares through a discount broker (like the previously mentioned Charles Schwab & Co.).

The following websites offer excellent advice and information on DRIPs: www.microinvesting.net/_wsn/page2.html; www.drip-central.com; www.dripinvestor.com; www.mreic.com/landy.html; www.fool.com/DRIPPort/whataredrips.htm.

TAKING ACTION

If you're looking to buy one share to enroll in a company's DRIP, consider First Share.

If you are truly interested in stock investing for as little money as possible, you want to buy as few shares as you can in order to qualify for participation in a company's DRIP. As I mentioned, you can buy your initial shares from a discount broker to get started. If you really want to buy just one share, I have a better idea: Go to First Share.

First Share is a program which specializes in permitting DRIP-minded investors to purchase single shares of stock. The costs associated with this program are very reasonable: Current sign-up cost is $24. Paying this fee puts you in the system and allows you to trade single shares of stock with other First Share members. Every time you make a transaction, total costs will run you about $12 (this, of course, excludes the cost of a share of the stock you're interested in). If you would like to know more about First Share, you may contact the company at 719-783-2929.

TAKING ACTION
Learn to use professional money-management techniques.

Okay, you've purchased your investments. Much to your surprise, you're already building a true portfolio of your very own and can see that your goals and dreams might actually become a reality! However, you're not satisfied. You know that there are a lot of investment professionals who know specialized money-management techniques to enhance returns, but you can't avail yourself of their services because you don't have enough money for them to manage. Are you left out in the cold? Can you benefit from these money-management techniques to enhance your returns? Yes—but you have to be willing to do some homework.

Time and space constraints don't allow me to venture into an in-depth discussion of artful money-management strategies, but I will offer a rudimentary explanation of the two most basic forms of money management, and I'll show you how you can implement each one in your portfolio. The first one is *fundamental analysis;* the second is *technical analysis.*

Fundamental Analysis

Fundamental analysts concern themselves with a company's earnings, sales, what it makes or what services it provides, and other similar elements. Fundamental analysis is the management of stocks and mutual funds through the evaluation of financial data that is specific to the companies being examined. Although it is possible to use fundamental analysis with respect to mutual fund management, it is more smartly used in connection with individual stocks.

One of the most important pieces of data which fundamental analysts examine when considering whether to buy or sell a particular stock is the *price-earnings (P/E) ratio.* This figure can be found in your newspaper stock tables. The P/E ratio is used to determine how to value a stock's prospects. A high P/E ratio, for example, means that its current price is much higher than its current earnings level, suggesting that investors are willing to pay in advance for a company they believe will shortly take off. By comparison, a low P/E ratio, which is made up of a stock price much closer in value to the earnings, suggests that investors don't expect much from the company in the near term. The only way to evaluate a P/E ratio is by comparing it to the P/Es of other companies that *make the same product or provide the same service.* You cannot, for example, compare the P/E of an auto maker with that of a restaurant chain.

In general, P/Es of 20 and above are regarded as being high, while P/Es of 10 and under are considered low. A P/E ratio between

10 and 20 is usually indicative of a perception of reasonable growth on the part of investors.

Well, you may be thinking, *this is easy; all I have to do is find the companies with the high P/Es* (and therefore the brightest futures) *and invest in those.* Not so fast. Remember, P/Es only indicate what investors *think* a company will do. Besides, if you buy a company with a high P/E, you're buying it at a relatively high price. The trick, then is to find the companies with low price-earnings ratios that nonetheless offer some evidence that they'll be doing much better soon.

Another element of fundamental analysis you want to be familiar with is the amount of a company's sales. When a company's sales increase, the gain in after-tax profit will either be paid out to investors in the form of dividends (more common in larger companies) or reinvested right back into the company to fund continued growth and expansion (more common in smaller companies). So, it's a good idea to begin tracking your prospective stock purchases on the basis of sales.

You should also watch dividend activity when looking at a company. If you're considering larger, well-known companies, you need to watch for an increase or decrease in the *dividend yield.* If the dividend yield of a larger company starts moving downward, it may be an indication that it's heading for tough times. However, be advised that smaller companies which may have excellent growth prospects do not usually pay sizable dividends, so dividend yield may not be as much of a consideration with those companies. One thing you can do is to watch the dividend yields of market indices as a whole for some guidance. For example, you'll find that the best times to buy are when the dividend yields of major indices like the Dow Jones Industrial Average and the S&P 500 are at 5% or greater, while the worst times are when the yields are at 3% or below. The former is an indicator that a down, or "bear," market has just ended. The latter tends to indicate that an up, or "bull," market has just come to an end.

Another fundamental indicator that you can use is the analysis of interest rates. Although interest rates pertain to the economy as a whole, their movement and level have an effect on companies everywhere. When interest rates are low, that's good news for corporations, because it means it will cost them less to borrow for expansion purposes. By contrast, higher interest rates force companies to pay a lot more for the same borrowed money, which means that borrowing will eat more heavily into their bottom line and lessen profits.

Trips to the library become important when you want to employ fundamental analysis as cost-effectively (read "cheaply") as possible. You should become familiar with financial trade papers such as the *Wall Street Journal* (which comes out daily; www.wsj.com/public/us) and *Barron's* (which is published weekly; www.barrons.com). Both papers are excellent sources of the kind of data you'll be looking for. (The excellent "Market Laboratory" section in *Barron's* provides very useful statistical data.) You should also be able to glean some of your needed information from your local newspaper, as long as it is not too small in scope. Beyond these resources, become familiar with the *Value Line* reports. These are one-page reports which offer a complete run-down on virtually every viable, publicly traded company (and its representative stock). The *Value Line* reports come out weekly, and any library worth its salt will carry them in its business reference section.

Technical Analysis

In contrast to fundamental analysis, technical analysts care little or nothing for the so-called fundamentals of a company.

They do not concern themselves with what a company makes, its records of sales, earnings, dividend payments, or anything else you would likely find on a balance sheet or annual report. Technical analysis is the study of the historical price movement of stocks or mutual funds for the purpose of predicting their movement in the future. Technical analysts rely heavily on tools such as charts and graphs to plot the price action of stocks and funds they're watching. At the core of the technical analyst's belief is the notion that it is market activity as a whole, as opposed to a company's inherent performance in particular, which is of greater importance. Technical analysis has evolved into a complex area of study through the years, and the advent of computers has given technicians the perfect tool for "crunching" data and tracking prices. However, it is possible for you to perform technical analysis on your own without spending a great deal of money. In fact, one of the most commonly used forms of technical analysis requires nothing more than a pencil, a piece of paper, and access to a newspaper on a weekly basis. Let's take a look.

Moving averages are perhaps the most basic and most easily understood of the technical analysis tools. A moving average is a running average of a stock or mutual fund's price over a set length of time. For example, a 10-week moving average is the average price of a security determined by averaging its weekly price over the previous ten weeks. The average "moves" because, as the weeks progress, the oldest price is dropped from the average and the newest (or most recent) price is calculated in. Although it doesn't matter what day of the week you select to get the prices for your average, it's best to be consistent. Many people, for example, like to use a security's weekly closing price for their average.

Now that you know what a moving average is, you're probably wondering what to do with it. The reason people calculate a moving average is to give them information necessary for making wise buy-and-sell decisions. Specifically, you compare the average price of the security you're watching with its price at the moment. In general, if the price of the security drops below the price of its average, that is a "sell" signal. By contrast, if the price rises above that of its average, this is regarded as a "buy" signal. So, if you're considering a particular mutual fund and have constructed a moving average, you'll be watching to see if its current price moves above its average price. If it does, you'll buy into the fund.

One of the nice things about moving averages is that they're easy to calculate. Once you've selected some funds or stocks to watch, simply assemble the moving averages based on the number of weeks or days you want to use (for mutual funds, relying on weekly prices is more than sufficient). The longer the term you select (like 30 weeks, for example), the more conservative your average will be; the shorter the term (5 or 10 weeks), the more aggressive it will be. Moving averages of a longer length may have you making exchanges more frequently.

To get started, pick some funds you'd like to consider. Once that's done, construct your averages. If you decide on a 10-week average, for example, you will have to obtain the closing prices for the fund on a particular day of the week for the last 10 weeks. (This may require a short trip to the library.) However, once your moving average is in place, you need only keep pace with the next week's closing price to recalculate the average and keep it current. Remember, as you add in the new figure you need to drop the oldest price. If you don't, your average will be for more than 10 weeks.

This is technical analysis in a nutshell. There are many fine books (and even a few periodicals) dedicated to the subject. You might be interested in perusing their contents as you find your interest in this area growing. You don't need to pay a money manager in order to enjoy the benefits of true investment strategies! All you need is resolve.

I have spoken only of stocks and stock mutual funds in this chapter because it has been shown that, over time, these investments are the most successful growth securities. It is possible, for example, to purchase U.S. Savings Bonds from your local bank for as little as $25 a shot, and I suppose we could have talked about that, but why? Savings Bonds may provide a lot of safety, but they do so at the significant expense of growth.

You now have a good head start to get you on the road to investment success. You don't have to be a rich person to "play the market"; you just need to know where to go and what to do. From here on out, you will be limited only by yourself.

Don't Give the IRS
All Your Money!

I f you earn very little money, it becomes incumbent upon you to try to keep as much as possible from slipping through your fingers. While the payment of taxes may not qualify as being a good example of money "slipping through one's fingers" in many people's minds, the truth is that there are solid ways for you to limit your tax burden significantly *without* cheating or refraining altogether from paying your taxes.

TAKING ACTION
No matter what...file!

Too many people, when faced with the reality of having insufficient funds to pay their April 15 income-tax bill, opt to simply not file. Let's be clear about this: The worst thing you can do when it comes to the Internal Revenue Service is to not file an income-tax return. You should never view filing as an option because it's not. While it's true that people who don't meet certain minimum income requirements don't have to file, you have to be at true poverty level in order to qualify.

Many people decide each year that they're not going to pay their taxes for one reason or another. Some people make the claim that the filing of taxes violates their religious beliefs, while others maintain that the government has no right to tax in the first place. The clear majority of nonfilers, however, are average people with average beliefs and sensibilities who simply choose not to file, believing they won't be noticed. The truth is that there have been a lot of court challenges to the requirement that the citizenry be required to file a tax return, but none have been successful. I wouldn't hold your breath that any of them ever will be. As soon as Uncle Sam deems any reason or circumstance worthy of excusing a citizen from filing a tax return, you'll have people all over the country doing their very best to meet the requirement—whatever it happens to be.

A lot of people who don't file aren't noticed, at least right away, but the situation tends to snowball. Once you choose not to file one year, you have made it tough on yourself if you decide to file in the future. What happens next is that many of the folks in this situation find themselves outside the taxpaying mainstream and unable to break back in. As time goes by, paranoia sets in, and these people find themselves limiting their involvement in society as a whole in an effort to avoid being caught by the tax-man.

The IRS views a fraudulent and willful failure to file as one of the greatest offenses that a citizen can commit against the agency (and the government). If you file late, you'll pay 5% of what you owe (in total) for each month you're late. This sum can go as high as 25% of the taxes you owe. On top of this, you'll likely be hit with interest and penalties. If you file a return but can't afford to pay your tax bill, you must pay one-half percent each month on the outstanding balance, up to 25% of the total owed. However, as bad as all of this seems, this is nothing compared to what you'll face if you're caught by the IRS for willful failure to file.

You could find yourself paying as much as an additional 75% of the amount of your tax bill. *Plus, you could face some time in jail!*

If the only reason you're thinking of not filing is because you fear you won't have enough money to pay your taxes, you should know that the IRS lets people who are in this situation make monthly payments on their tax bill. If you've calculated your taxes for a given year and find that your bank account will be short what you need to pay the bill, you have the option of calling the IRS and requesting that they let you pay off your obligation in installments. As long as you are up-to-date on all of your other tax obligations for previous tax years and are making regular tax payments currently (through withholding or estimated tax payments), your request to pay off your outstanding tax bill through the use of a payment plan will likely be approved. I know people who are on this type of plan with the IRS, and they report having no problems. According to them, they aren't hassled in any way. In fact, they don't even hear from the IRS beyond their receipt of a monthly statement that shows how much money they have left to pay off. (It also includes an envelope in which to return the payment!)

There's really nothing to be afraid of when dealing with the IRS. The key is to always be up front and aboveboard in your dealing with them—and that includes making sure you file a return each year.

TAKING ACTION
Beware of rapid refund services.

We've all seen them. The ads from various tax preparation services that announce you can receive your refund on the spot if you let them file your return for you. However, know that what is *not* going on is the IRS immediately processing your return and speeding your refund back to you in minutes. (This is the federal government we're talking about!) What *is* going on is that the tax preparation service, which touts the rapid refund, files your return electronically. Then, having verification from the return that you will be receiving a refund and how much it is, they *loan* you the amount of your expected windfall right then and there. When your actual refund arrives from the IRS, it is collected by the preparation service.

One thing you should always keep in mind is that if someone or some company advertises that they can provide a service for you faster and more quickly, you can bet it's going to cost you more as well. That rule is true with respect to rapid refunds. Because you're receiving a loan from the preparation service in lieu of the actual refund money, you'll find yourself paying interest . . . high interest. In fact, the effective interest rate paid on such loans by consumers is often as high as 30%, and it can be more. So, unless you are in urgent need of the money and absolutely cannot wait a few weeks for your genuine refund, my suggestion would be to put the exorbitant interest charges back into your pocket and wait for the mailperson to deliver the real deal to you or use automatic deposit. As time goes on, it's likely that one day you'll be able to file electronically on your own for free. Until that day arrives, steer clear of the electronic filing/rapid refund arrangement.

TAKING ACTION
Adjust your withholding
so that you eliminate your refund.

Having just read the title of this principle, you may be thinking, *What? Why in the world would I want to get rid of my annual refund? Doesn't he understand? I need money; that's why I'm reading this book.* Relax. I'm not suggesting that you do away with your refund; I'm suggesting that you get it earlier in the year when it will do you more good. Let me explain.

Whenever you watch TV at tax time, you're likely to run across commercials put on by the big tax-preparation services enticing you to have your taxes prepared by them. One of the favorite strategies they employ in their commercials is to have apparently satisfied customers talk about what a big refund the company got for them the previous year. It sounds great, doesn't it? I mean, we'd all like to get a big tax refund from Uncle Sam, wouldn't we?

Well, when you realize just what a tax refund is, it's really not so exciting. A tax refund is, as the word "refund" should so clearly indicate, nothing more than a return of taxes which you overpaid during the past year through your withholding or through the estimated taxes you paid if you are self-employed. It is not, as some people have apparently conned themselves into thinking, a windfall of extra money that just happens to come your way. The significance of this is that you are entitled to this money long before you get it back from the IRS. To put this money back into your pocket a lot sooner, simply go down to your company's payroll department and ask to complete a new W-4 form. The W-4 tells the payroll clerks how much of your check to withhold for the payment of taxes. You filled it out when you first started. If you've been getting sizable refunds each tax season, you've declared too few exemptions and should declare more. Your goal is to have the right amount of taxes taken out each pay period so that when April 15 comes, you have a zero balance on your tax return. You don't owe; you don't receive a refund. It is sometimes difficult to hit a zero balance exactly, but you want to come as close as possible.

Obviously, when you adjust your withholding you get your "refund" all year long in the form of a larger paycheck. This is very prudent from a money-management standpoint. For example, the extra money in your paycheck can be used to initiate or even increase your monthly investment into your mutual fund account. By using your money this way, not only do you see the refund sooner but you put it to work, making it grow all year long. The IRS does that as well, of course, but you don't get the interest at the end of the year along with your refund. They keep the interest; you just get the refund.

TAKING ACTION

If you are a low-income family, make sure you take the earned income credit.

If you don't have any money because you don't make much money (as opposed to having a plethora of bills draining your otherwise-plentiful resources), you need to find the breaks where you can. If you fit the IRS's definition of a low-income family, make sure you take one of the few tax credits left available to Americans.

It should be said right up from that a *tax credit* beats a *tax deduction* any day of the week. A tax deduction lowers your tax bill in proportion to your tax bracket. A tax credit, however, gives you a dollar-for-dollar reduction in your tax bill. There aren't many tax credits left. Most Americans with average incomes and at least one child can qualify to take the credit for dependent and child-care expenses. (If you pay for more than half of the expenses of a child or other dependent, you are eligible to take a tax credit. The amount is determined by your annual income.) There are also tax credits available for people who make investments in certain kinds of housing, but if you don't have much money investing probably isn't one of your usual habits. Fortunately, the most lucrative (relatively speaking) tax credit which is still available to folks is available only to low-income families. It is the earned income credit.

The earned income credit can significantly reduce your tax burden. It can even provide you with a refund if you make too little money to owe taxes! (This may be the closest thing to an exception to what I said earlier about the refund being an overpayment of taxes and not a windfall of extra money.) For the tax year 2002, the credit was as much as $4,140 if you had more than one child, as much as $2,506 if you had one child, and as much as $376 if you had no children. To qualify in 2002, your income, if you had more than one child, could not be more than $34,178; if you had one child, it could not be more than $30,201; if you had no children, it could not be more than $12,060. One thing I should point out is that these income limitations refer to a combination of taxable as well as nontaxable earned income. Examples of nontaxable income are contributions to company retirement plans, military housing benefits, and subsistence funds.

It is believed that many people who qualify don't take the earned income credit. There are probably a lot of reasons for this, but one surely has to do with the fact that the people who qualify for this credit oftentimes make too little to pay taxes. They probably don't get far enough into the process to see that there's a credit for them to take. Too bad, because the money would obviously help. If your income is in the ranges quoted above, there's a good chance you will be able to take the earned income credit. Make certain the next time you go to fill out your taxes that you've taken the time to review the qualifications for the earned income credit to see if you can take it. This is probably the best deal available on the income tax for low-income folks—and it may be the best deal available period. You can call the IRS at 1-800-829-1040 for more information.

TAKING ACTION
Deductions...take 'em!

In the last principle I talked about how the tax credit is superior to the deduction for the individual taxpayer. Nonetheless, you should take deductions where you can. In my opinion, too many people are shy about claiming deductions on their tax returns. If you don't have much money, you cannot afford to be shy or nonchalant. Approach the claiming of deductions aggressively, but with preparation and forethought. This means that you should not take them haphazardly. Whenever you take a deduction, you need to be able to back up your claim with documentation. To put it another way, don't expect the IRS to take your word for the fact that you're eligible for the deduction you're claiming. Record keeping is not difficult, but it can be a little tedious at times. If claiming deductions puts more money back in your pocket, what's a little inconvenience now and again?

The key to winning the deductions game is to have itemized deductions which exceed your *standard* deduction. The standard deduction is the portion of your income on which you don't pay taxes. Everyone qualifies for it. Your goal is to have the sum of your *itemized* deductions exceed the standard deduction which applies in your case. In general, the deductions you can take will be indicated on "Schedule A" that goes along with your Form 1040. Let's take a look at some of the more common deductions you may qualify to take:

- *unreimbursed medical expenses*—they must exceed 7.5% of your adjusted gross income. The range of medical expenses that you can deduct is very wide. You are only prohibited from deducting those expenses that are not directly related to the payment of medical services, procedures, or prescriptions.

- *state and local taxes*

- *interest on your home mortgage*

- *property taxes*

- *contributions to organizations* that have as their stated purpose religious, charitable, educational, scientific, or literary endeavors

- *contributions to organizations* that work to prevent cruelty to children or animals

- *losses incurred* as a result of theft, vandalism, fire, storm, or other bona fide casualties

Each of these categories of deductions has specific rules and parameters which pertain to them. You would do well to contact the IRS for more information, although a lot of what you need to know can be found within the instruction book for the Form 1040.

This is just the tip of the iceberg for deductions. Now it gets interesting. We just finished examining the categories of deductions that most of us can qualify to take at one time or another. Now we want to take a look at that famous category of deductions that can really help you out, but that takes some planning and attention to detail to exploit: miscellaneous deductions.

There are a lot of additional expenses, beyond those mentioned above, that the IRS has declared deductible. However, most of these cannot be deducted in full. You are required to subtract 2% of your adjusted gross income from the sum total of these deductions. For example, let's say that your adjusted gross income is $20,000. You may deduct all of the qualified expenses that are greater than 2% of $20,000, or $400. In general, the expenses that most regularly qualify as deductions in this category are those that have to do with the commission of your job and are not reimbursed. Examples of these are:

- travel—transportation, meals, and entertainment expenses

- union dues

- equipment you need to do your job

- uniforms

- protective clothing

- physical examinations required by your employer

- subscriptions to professional organizations and publications

- moving expenses incurred when you take a new job

There are other job-related expenses that are deductible, but this list gives you a pretty good idea of the expenses that usually fall under the heading "miscellaneous deductions."

There are also a handful of expenses that qualify as miscellaneous deductions that aren't necessarily job-related, most notably the payment of fees for investment advice and tax preparation. There are even some deductible expenses that are not subject to the 2% "floor." You can consult the instruction book for Form 1040 for a full listing.

Remember, strive to qualify for and take as many deductions as you can. If you keep good records and take only those deductions for which you truly qualify, you will never have any problems.

TAKING ACTION
Always complete the 1040 long form.

The Form 1040 is the longest and most tedious of the common income tax forms that you will ever have to complete. However, if you want to put as much money as possible back into your pocket, this is the only form for you. The 1040 is designed for people who wish to take as many deductions as possible. While you're completing the form, it refers you to other accompanying forms for deductions you may be able to take. Even if you are not eligible for the deductions outlined in these other sections, look and see where possible deductions might exist for the future. When you complete the long form, you are guaranteed to pay less in taxes.

The short forms might be tempting to use since they are much simpler and quicker to complete. They *do not* allow you to take the deductions available if you go with the longer form. When you use the short form, you always pay the maximum tax possible. Is that what you really want to do? Although the completion of the Form 1040 is a bit more complicated and time-consuming, it could put hundreds—even thousands—of dollars back in your pocket!

TAKING ACTION

Do your own taxes— it's easier than you think.

Many people are tempted to have their taxes prepared by an outside source, such as a tax preparation service, an accountant, or a brother-in-law. They believe that doing taxes is too complicated an endeavor for them. If you have someone else do your taxes for you, how do you know you're getting all the help and wisdom to which you're entitled? If you remain unfamiliar with how the tax-preparation process works, you'll never know what's going on or what's to your advantage or disadvantage. The only way you'll know is to do your own taxes. It's not difficult, and the instructions that are provided by the IRS for each of the applicable forms are surprisingly clear and straightforward.

One of the dark secrets of tax preparation services is that you may not always get all the deductions for which you're eligible. This can be especially true if you have your taxes prepared at the height of tax season. Preparers who are overworked and paid in part by the number of returns they complete may choose alternatives for some deductions that won't save you as much money. For example, there are alternatives for automobile, interest, and investment deductions that can save a preparer time but which will not save you as much money. Even if you insist on using a preparer, you should at least check his work yourself to be certain you're getting all the deductions you deserve.

TAKING ACTION

Use a tax preparer only if you are confident that you'll save money.

I've already mentioned that the preparation of individual tax returns is not nearly as difficult as some would lead you to believe. Nevertheless, a majority of Americans use tax preparers. As our tax code becomes increasingly involved and convoluted, many more will. As a result, it seems that tax preparation is becoming a growth industry.

Unfortunately, a lot of tax preparers are not as aggressive as they should be in their pursuits. They're easily intimidated by the tax code and tend to overcompensate by neglecting to claim deductions on your behalf that would put more money back in your pocket. This is perhaps the biggest problem with using a tax preparation service. If you walk in and let someone you've never spoken to or seen before work on your taxes, you have no idea if you're involved with a smart, aggressive preparer or one who is there to complete as many returns as possible (because that's how he gets paid). I'm not necessarily foursquare against the use of a tax preparer, but the choice to do so must come down to a simple matter of economics: When it's all said and done, will you end up with more money back in your pocket if you go with a preparer, or will you have more if you complete the return yourself? If you're not convinced that the preparer will beat the results you could achieve on your own by at least the margin of his fee, prepare the return yourself.

There are a lot of preparation services out there. If you do consider having someone else prepare your return for you, I would recommend going to a source other than the usual, well-known services like H.R. Block, Jackson Hewitt, and the rest. In general, the preparers who work there are laypeople who have completed a short, in-house course on tax preparation. That's certainly better than nothing, but it hardly qualifies one as an expert in the tax code and, more importantly, in dealing with the IRS.

Any preparer you consider should be well-versed in the policies, procedures, and yes, even the temperament, of the Internal Revenue Service. To that end, I recommend that you look to a kind of preparer known as an *enrolled agent*. An enrolled agent is a licensed taxpayer representative who offers tax advice and can prepare returns. To become an enrolled agent, one must pass a strenuous examination administered by the IRS. Many EAs have previously worked as IRS auditors.

There is a National Association of Enrolled Agents. If you contact them, they will send you the names of three enrolled agents who live near you. You may reach the Association at 200 Orchard Ridge Drive, Suite 302, Gaithersburg, MD 20878-1978. Their telephone numbers are 800-424-4339 / 301-212-9608 / Fax 301-990-1611 / e-mail naea1@aol. com.

TAKING ACTION
Reduce your chances of being audited by filing later.

Tax audits are never enjoyable experiences. Even if everything you've put down as a deduction is completely aboveboard and verifiable, the grilling can be very worrisome and stressful.

Therefore, you should take whatever reasonable steps you can to avoid being audited. One great way to do that is to file your tax return as late as possible. Many people pride themselves on doing their taxes early, getting them out of the way and moving on to bigger and better things. People who expect to receive a refund really love to file early, because they're dying to get that check from Uncle Sam. That is great—except for one thing: If you file early, your chances of being audited rise dramatically.

The IRS has long maintained that such is not the case, but it is. The IRS's computers select the returns to be audited based on the number that was programmed into them for that particular year, as well as on the specific criteria that make up each deduction category from which returns are to be selected. Once that number of returns has been met in each category, guess what? No more returns will be selected. Remember, auditors are human beings and, much to the IRS's chagrin I'm sure, humans can't work as fast as their computer counterparts that select the returns to begin with. So, yes, there is a limit to the number of returns that will be audited in any given year. That number is determined by the higher-ups at the Internal Revenue Service. Just play the numbers game. File your return as late as possible—right up until midnight of April 15. This strategy doesn't necessarily guarantee that you won't be audited, but it does reduce your chances significantly.

TAKING ACTION

Don't let the IRS use your refund.

When you get to the end of your Form 1040, you will have an option to apply your refund (assuming you're getting one) to next year's taxes. Lots of people do it, figuring that it will relieve them from next year's misery. The IRS loves it when you elect to do this because it gives them the use of *your* money for an additional year. What are the problems associated with this? If you received a refund this year, there's probably a reasonable chance that you'll receive one next year. Second, if you're receiving a refund, it means you've been overpaying your taxes for the previous year. The IRS has already been enjoying the use of your money for over a year (the previous calendar year and the first few months of the current year). Don't give them the free use of your money for over two years!

If you are content to forego the active use of this refund money for another year, you can put it in your own investment account and keep the growth or the interest for yourself. Giving the IRS use of your money for an extra year is clearly a losing proposition, especially for anyone who is short of money.

TAKING ACTION
Turn your long-term investments into tax-deferred retirement plans.

Whether you have a lot of money or a little money, if you invest in fully taxable brokerage or mutual fund accounts you will be required to pay capital gains taxes each year. If you've been able to pick some real winners, and the value of your choices rises sharply, you may find yourself owing Uncle Sam more than you expected. The beauty of investing in regular, fully taxable accounts is that you have access to your money without restriction. Retirement accounts (like IRAs) force you to abide by strict rules regarding access to the money in the plans. They impose significant penalties if you *do* choose to slip your hand into the cookie jar. However, if your investment plans are long-term (like shooting for a comfortable, worry-free retirement), then you probably don't have much to fear from the IRS's penalties with respect to your retirement account.

All working Americans who have earned income may set up their own tax-deferred retirement plans. Depending on their incomes, these plans can provide a sizable deduction from their annual income-tax liability. These plans are called Individual Retirement Plans (IRAs). Each working American may deposit up to $3,500 of earned income into his (or her) IRA each year. Plus, if he meets certain income limitation requirements, he may be able to deduct all of his annual contribution on his income taxes. You may open an IRA at any bank, brokerage house, or mutual fund company. There are also special trustees that will house your IRA. (Trustees sometimes allow you to deposit unusual investments into your tax-deferred account.)

The chief advantage offered by the IRA is tax-deferral. Rather than face ongoing capital gains liabilities that result from your investment successes, you sidestep that by doing your buying and selling within an account that allows you to forego current tax obligations. It is only when you pull money out of the account—when you retire—that you have to pay taxes. By then, you will probably be in a lower tax bracket, which increases your benefit further. Tax-deferral is a winning influence on investments. Rather than being slowed by the annual bite of capital gains taxes, your investments enjoy uninterrupted growth at a rate that cannot be matched outside of a tax-deferred account. IRS publication 590 explains IRAs.

Another great advantage to IRAs that, unfortunately, cannot be enjoyed by all account owners is the ability to deduct your annual IRA contribution from your income tax. The government wants to encourage citizens to rely on themselves when retirement day comes so that the burden to the U.S. taxpayer is held in check. An incentive they offer is to allow people to deduct their annual contributions. If you are single you may deduct your entire contribution. If you are married filing jointly you may deduct the full amount of your contributions. If you or your spouse contribute to a company-sponsored retirement plan where you work, your eligibility to deduct your annual IRA contribution may be completely eliminated. IRS Publication 590 and your Form 1040 instruction book provide worksheets and information to help you determine how much, if any, of your contribution you may deduct.

This is a great tax break for investment-minded folks. They enjoy the double benefit of avoiding ongoing capital gains liabilities and realizing the ability to deduct their contributions from their annual taxes.

The biggest disadvantage to housing your investments inside tax-deferred accounts is that you have very restricted access to the money. If you withdraw any of the money before you reach age 59½, you generally must pay a 10% excise tax on what you've withdrawn. The withdrawn money also becomes taxable as ordinary income for that year. For this reason, you must be pretty sure you're going to be able to stay invested for the long haul. If you are, it's a great way to see a better, faster return on your money and significantly lower your annual tax liability.

TAKING ACTION

Turn your losing stock or mutual fund into a winning tax advantage.

Although I've just finished talking up the benefits of keeping your investments housed in a tax-deferred retirement account whenever possible, you also want to keep some of your money in a fully taxable brokerage or mutual fund account. Many people like the fact that they can access their money without any trouble in such accounts, so they typically have one of each. While there really isn't any definable tax advantage to maintaining a fully taxable investment account, if you pick a stock or fund that performs poorly therein, there's a way to turn that losing position into a tax advantage.

Let's say you get to the end of a calendar year and notice that you have three stocks or funds that have increased nicely in value from the date of purchase. You also have one that has lost a fair amount of value from its original purchase date. You choose to sell one of your winning positions because you feel it has run its course and you want to lock in your gains. The only thing stopping you is that you know you'll be faced with paying a capital gains tax. If you sell your losing position before the end of the year as well, you can offset your gain in the one position by the amount of your loss in the other. This works for up to $3,000. If your loss exceeds $3,000, you can carry that excess over into the next year, and do the same thing. Furthermore, if your losses exceed your gains—or if you have no gains at all—you can deduct that capital loss from your ordinary income. Check out IRS publication 544 for more information.

TAKING ACTION

When given the choice,
choose employer-sponsored benefits
over an increase in salary.

When most people consider compensation, they focus on salary or wages. Sure, a benefits package is considered relevant, but in general people think about their compensation in terms of salary. That being said, what's the best way to boost your after-tax income? Receive a raise or pick up a few additional employee benefits? The answer is to pick up your increase in the form of benefits. Remember that, ultimately, after-tax income is the only thing that matters.

When you receive health care benefits paid by your employer as part of your compensation, they're usually tax-free. Now, you might be thinking, *Well, what difference does this make? After all, unreimbursed medical expenses are tax-deductible, so I win either way, right?* Wrong. First of all, you can only deduct medical expenses that exceed 7.5% of your adjusted gross income. Second, deductions for expenses you've incurred will never compare to having the whole expense paid for. If an employer does not currently offer a health plan, there are a couple of types he might consider implementing. The first one is known as a *medical expense reimbursement plan*; the second is an *insured medical plan.* With the medical expense reimbursement plan, the employee is allowed to defer, pretax, a portion of his check into a special account out of which his medical costs will be reimbursed. The insured medical plan is more like the kinds of health coverage we normally think about as being offered through employers. Another option you have is to ask your employer to reimburse you for the cost of the health coverage you've gone out and picked up on your own.

Let's say you have children and require the services of a daycare facility. If you're not lucky enough to have an employer-sponsored daycare program where you work, no problem. Ask your employer to pick up the expenses of daycare in your behalf in lieu of a raise. If you have children and work, you know how much of a drain daycare can be on your financial resources. If daycare costs you $100 per week per child, and you have two children, you're paying roughly $10,000 per year in daycare costs. What would you rather have *now*—a raise or employer-sponsored/reimbursed daycare?

I've found in my travels that a lot of people out there qualify for tax-free, employer-paid meals and/or lodging. To be tax-free, the benefits have to be provided for the convenience of the employer and must be provided on the employer's premises. If you work in a restaurant, for example, tax-free meals are probably available to you anytime you want them. Frequently, people who work in the hotel business or who work for apartment complexes obtain their lodging as part of their compensation. Furthermore, it should be mentioned that when lodging qualifies as being free, associated living expenses such as the cost of utilities are tax-free as well.

One way to deal with these expenses is to ask your employer to set up an expense reimbursement plan. Any unreimbursed employment-related expenses that you incur are deductible. But, as I've mentioned already, deductions are not as beneficial as tax-saving mechanisms such as credits and expenses that are reimbursed by employers. And itemized miscellaneous deductions are subject to the 2% "floor" that I mentioned in the section on deductions. However, if your employer sets up what is called an "accountable plan," you can have your expenses reimbursed tax-free. With an accountable plan, you turn in your receipts and other relevant records regarding employment-related expenses that you've incurred, and the employer reimburses you. Not only do these reimbursements not count toward income taxes, they also aren't counted for payroll taxes.

I've mentioned just a few of the expenses that can rightfully be subject to tax-free employer reimbursement. To get your hands on a thorough source of information with respect to these deductions (and more ideas about the expenses that are ripe for reimbursement), call the IRS at 800-TAX-FORMS and request Publication 529, "Miscellaneous Deductions," and Publication 535, "Business Expenses."

TAKING ACTION

If you're a homeowner, make sure you're not paying too much in property taxes.

Property tax funds are used by local counties and municipalities to raise money for projects, services, and other areas of concern covered by local governments. Public works maintenance and the operation of local public schools are two examples of the activities financed substantially by property-tax revenue. For the purposes of determining what your property taxes are going to be in the coming year, your home will be subject to an annual property tax assessment. The assessment is your local county's or municipality's statement of the value of your home. Obviously, the higher the assessment, the higher your property taxes will be.

Frequently, you'll hear of neighbors, perhaps friends or acquaintances of yours, who protest the assessments on their homes. There seems to be a lot of disagreements in communities all over the country as to the assessments made by local property appraisers. Obviously, local government has a vested interest in seeing that your property value increases, because it means they will realize more money through taxes. You have to be vigilant and make sure that the city or county doesn't decide that your residence is worth more than it really is.

If you don't know if the county or city has issued a fair assessment of the value of your house—find out! Your first step is to find out your home's official assessed value. (This is on your tax statement.) Next, multiply this value, also called the "fair market value," by the assessment ratio that applies to your community. If you have the money and seriously doubt the accuracy of your community's assessment, it would be a good idea to have an independent commercial appraisal done on your home that will (hopefully) back up your claim. Additionally, you would be wise to contact a local real-estate agent who has knowledge of the prices that comparable homes in your neighborhood have sold for recently. Use those prices to help determine whether or not your assessment is too high. Finally, you can go down to your city or town hall and look up the assessed values of your neighbors' homes to help give you some guidance that way as well. (Some information may also be available on the internet.) Once you have assembled a body of evidence that backs up your claim that your assessment is too high, contact the appropriate local authority and inquire as to how you may initiate a formal protest. If you are successful, your assessment will be adjusted downward—as will your property taxes.

TAKING ACTION

Lower your taxes by starting a small business.

Flat out, I think one of the best tax shelters available that's accessible to just about all Americans—regardless of income—is the small business. The beauty of the small business, from the standpoint of taxation, is that any of the personal items you own or things you do are partially to fully deductible as long as they're used or done in the business. What's more, these miscellaneous expenses, which normally cannot be deducted unless they exceed the 2% floor, can be deducted without qualification as long as they're considered business deductions.

At this point, you may be thinking, *A small business? How am I going to start a business? Not only would I need a lot of money to start a business, I have too many responsibilities to leave my current position to pursue that option.* Not true! Although you will need some money and the dedication, discipline, and responsibility that goes with starting a new business, it's not imposible. A small business can be run out of your home on a part-time basis—even with that level of operation you enjoy all the tax benefits of owning and running a business that the big companies do.

The easiest type of business to set up is a sole proprietorship. You don't have to complete any special forms or applications to set up a sole proprietorship, and you don't have to worry about adhering to any special, complex tax laws. With a sole proprietorship, your social security number serves as the Tax I.D. number for the business. Instead of filling out a bunch of special forms at tax time for your business, you just fill out Schedule C, Profit or Loss from Business (Sole Proprietorship), which goes along with your Form 1040. Because they don't require any special procedures or major expenses to start up, sole proprietorships are ideal for small, home-based businesses. It should be noted that you don't enjoy the same protection from liability that a corporation does, but if your business remains low-profile that won't become an issue. If your business does grow to the point where you would like to dedicate all of your time to its operation, then you can worry about incorporating.

The best thing about having a business with respect to tax benefits is that in the first couple of years of operation, you don't have to make any money to earn your deductions. In fact, if your expenses exceed your income, the resulting loss (which will be indicated on Schedule C) will go toward lowering your personal tax liability by decreasing your personal income. In other words, if you earn $20,000 this year at your full-time, salaried job, but report a loss in your small business of $2,000, your total income drops to $18,000 for tax purposes. However, if your business does not show a profit in either of the first two years of operation, you may lose the privilege of deducting your expenses. This has to do with the "three out of five" rule, which states that your business must show a profit in any three out of five years. If that happens, though, you can simply start another business. Your "three out of five" ruling period begins all over with the inception of the new business. For more information on this subject, call the IRS at 800-TAX-FORMS and request Publication 334, "Tax Guide for Small Business."

Fun and a Budget
Can Coexist

Whenever we're short on cash, we have to decide what we're going to keep and what facets of our lives we're going to part with (at least for a while). Unfortunately, because having fun is rarely considered a necessity, any expenses related to entertainment are typically eliminated right off the bat.

This can be doubly painful for the family with very little money because they are usually the ones most in need of diversions. Working and worrying can put a tremendous strain on the spirit, and even the smallest bit of enjoyment can provide folks with a deep satisfaction and the will to persevere in the face of what often seems like an uphill battle.

Too often, we equate fun with activities such as going to expensive amusement parks (Disney World, for example) or attending professional major-league sporting events, where attendance for a family of four can cost well over $100. And that's before you've bought anything to eat! Granted, the fun you can have for just a few dollars may not be as spectacularly satisfying as watching big-time professional athletes battle it out or riding one of the many thrilling rides at Disney, but there's absolutely no reason why you can't go out, have fun, and give your mind and spirit a rest from the worries of the financial constraints in which you currently find yourself.

TAKING ACTION
Use entertainment coupon books.

I don't know if there are statistics kept on how often coupons are used to attend entertainment-based diversions like movies, concerts, and other such activities, but it doesn't seem like they're used very often. That's too bad because you can save a tremendous amount of money, which makes entertainment options that are normally cost-prohibitive accessible to everybody.

In our superficial, highly judgmental society, a lot of folks balk at using coupons because they don't want to be perceived as having too little money or being unwilling to spend what they do have. If you're one of these people, I have just one thing to say to you: Get over it! People cannot afford to be prideful to the point where they refuse to take advantage of the help coupons offer. Furthermore, that would be a case of foolish pride because people from all walks of life use coupons. Quite often, these little goodies allow a family to go out and enjoy themselves instead of having to stay home.

One of the best deals in coupons available anywhere is the *Entertainment '04* coupon books that are sold throughout the country. As the name suggests, the books give people many opportunities to save money on all sorts of entertainment and recreational activities. And many of the coupons offer "buy one, get one free" deals. These coupon books are usually sold through groups and organizations everywhere. The cost ranges from $25 to $45. If you would like to know more about how you can get your hands on one of these books, call Entertainment Publications at 800-477-3234. You may also write to them at P.O. Box 1068, Trumbull, CT 06611.

TAKING ACTION
Enjoy the big-screen movie experience at the discount theater.

These days you can find just about *anything* in a discounted form or version. As consumerism takes on an active life of its own, citizens all across this great land are demanding that providers of goods and services find a way to offer their wares to the public for less money. To that end, the discount movie theater has taken root in shopping malls and similar locations throughout the country. Discount movie theaters show movies on the big screen for prices that are deeply discounted from those found at the bigger, fancier theaters—oftentimes the cost is just $1 per ticket. The trade-off is that the films shown are not usually just-released, but are somewhere between the current, wide-release stage and the video stage. If you have one of these discount theaters located nearby, it is one of the best economic opportunities available to take the family to a full-size movie theater to enjoy films

TAKING ACTION
Rent your videos or CDs at the library.

Videocassette recorders and tapes or CD players and CDs have quickly become a staple of the American household. In fact, many people I know have a house rule that any movies to be watched will be rented because they are so disgusted with the prices of movie-theater tickets. Many people gravitate to videos/CDs because they like the idea of watching a movie in the comfort and safety of their own home—free from unanticipated distractions, crowds, and accessible to personal conveniences on their terms. However, even movie rentals can be too expensive for the thrifty consumer. One well-known rental company, for example, charges customers based on a three-night rental. That's great, but how often do you take three nights to watch a single movie?

The answer to this problem is your local library. Most libraries, which once had little more than a token video/CD section containing movies that were not terribly popular, have now added a much larger supply of desirable video/CD options. If you have a library card, you can "check out" movies! (If there is an additional charge, it's usually around $1.) Another solid advantage to heading to the library to rent videos/CDs is that it doesn't usually carry movies that would be considered objectionable for family viewing. Finally, libraries generally have rental policies that are more liberal than those of professional movie rental retailers, allowing cardholders to rent lots of movies at one time—and keep them for as long as a couple of weeks.

TAKING ACTION
Consider buying "previously viewed" videos/CDs.

Sometimes renting a video/CD just isn't enough. Every once in a while, a movie or presentation comes along and you just gotta have it. Unfortunately, new videos/CDs can cost a bundle.

You can get new movies in large, discount department stores such as K-Mart and Wal-Mart and pay less than you would if you bought them from specialty video/CD stores. Even then, you're paying more than you have to. To get your movie at an honest-to-goodness fair price, buy it secondhand. The smart way to do that—to ensure you're getting quality and a measure of protection—is to buy them from the movie-rental outfits. Many videos/CDs that were once on the shelves as rental copies are packaged by the stores and sold at a discount. These videos/CDs are usually labeled "previously viewed." They are normally in excellent condition, and they cost anywhere from $5 to $15—significantly less than their brand-new counterparts.

TAKING ACTION
Consider renting video games.

Ah, video games. It seems as though their popularity has subsided a bit, but they are still enjoyed by millions of Americans every day. The problem is, the individual games can be very expensive—some even close to the $100 mark! Even "average" video games can put you out $40 or so. The real problem with game videos is the "interest" factor. The interest that the newest, hottest games generate can subside relatively quickly—meaning they sit on the shelf gathering dust—and you're still out your purchase price.

The solution is to *rent* video games. Video-rental stores offer them just like they rent movies—and for about the same price. If you're convinced that you like a particular game well enough to buy it, then do so. However, renting is a nice way to enjoy a variety of games for the same price it would cost to purchase just one.

TAKING ACTION
Satisfy your craving to watch professional sports by attending minor-league games.

The level of athlete we all hear about and admire is the major-league professional. For basketball, they are the players of the National Basketball Association, for hockey, the National Hockey League, and for baseball it's Major League Baseball. Each one of these sports is represented by professional leagues in this country which are made up of either young, up-and-coming future major leaguers or people who have already spent some time at the top and are on their way down. While the talent level of the individual players is not usually on par with that of the top-level pros, the competitiveness can be just as fierce. And the truth is, the play is quite good. Best of all, the tickets to these minor-league games are considerably cheaper than those of the big leaguers. For the cost of one decent seat at a major-league baseball game, for example, you can take your family out to a minor league game *and* buy hotdogs and Cokes for everyone.

These games can be a lot of fun. The stadiums and arenas are usually a lot smaller, so there's more of an opportunity for communal spectator participation and enjoyment of the event. Your best opportunity to take part as a spectator in a minor-league professional game is probably in baseball. (There are a number of different levels of professional minor-league teams throughout the nation.) If you're not certain about the availability of a minor-league baseball team in your area, ask the National Association of Professional Baseball Leagues for assistance. They will send you a list of the teams that are located near you. Write to the association at P.O. Box A, St. Petersburg, Florida 33731.

TAKING ACTION
Look for discounts at athletic facilities.

If you're more of a doer than a watcher, then you'll want to keep your eyes peeled for discounts offered at athletic facilities. Ice skating, for example, is very popular even in parts of the country where it doesn't snow. Many rinks charge customers less during certain times of the day or on particular days when attendance tends to be low. Swimming pools and golf courses do the same thing, as do bowling alleys and rifle ranges. Many such athletic and sportsman facilities will have special rates for off-peak hours, which means you can indulge in your favorite sport without having to worry if you have enough money in your pocket. Find your favorite sporting locations in your area, and call to find out if they have price breaks for off-hours customers.

TAKING ACTION
Enjoy high-quality
concert music live and free!

Some of the most favored and popular forms of entertainment include symphony concerts put on by regional bands and orchestras and plays and productions put on by theater companies and dance troupes. Unfortunately, the price of tickets for these events can be princely, especially if the performance group in question is well-known and quite popular.

There *is* a way to see these wonderful performers in action without paying the established prices for the regularly scheduled performances. How? Simple—go to the rehearsals.

Many of these performance groups will admit the general public to witness their rehearsals for a price which is deeply discounted from that of a regular admission ticket. Some will even let the public come and watch free of charge. I'm not talking about just your local community theater plays or small-time performance groups. The biggies will let you do this as well. The New York Philharmonic, for example, is famous for allowing the general public to watch a set number of its rehearsals each season. At last check, ticket prices were just $14 apiece. The best way to track down these bargains is to locate the telephone numbers to the performance groups themselves or to the theaters and concert halls in which they perform, and then call. Ask if the group in question has any rehearsals that are accessible to the general public, and go from there. Again, this is an excellent, viable alternative to paying full price for official performances. All it takes is a little initiative.

TAKING ACTION

See plays without paying top-dollar for tickets.

A lot of people love the theater, but tickets to plays can be extraordinarily expensive—and not just for Broadway shows.

There are ways to get around forking over the big bucks and still get to see the shows you want. Let's look at a few of them.

Very often a theater company that has been rehearsing for weeks and months will offer opportunities for the public to attend preview showings of the play. The tickets to these preview shows do cost, and the performance may not be quite at the level which it will be when the play opens officially, but the prices are deeply discounted. As a result, it's a terrific bargain *and* an unbeatable opportunity for the penny-wise who love the theater. To find out more about preview showings, contact the theater where the play you'd like to see is scheduled to open.

Many special events have discounted tickets as the start time approaches, and plays are no different. If there are seats available before curtain time, the box office will usually make them available a half-hour or so before the play starts. To make sure of the availability of such tickets on the night you'd like to go, it would be wise to call the box office before you head down there—about an hour or so before the curtain is scheduled to go up. Use of this strategy, of course, involves a willingness to head out the door and to go to the theater at a moment's notice.

If you live in or around New York City, or plan to be there sometime in the future, it's possible to get a sensational deal on tickets to the headline shows that play on Broadway.

There are special coupons you can get that will allow you to secure two tickets to a Broadway show for the price of one. To obtain these valuable coupons, send a self-addressed, stamped envelope to Hit Show Club, 630 Ninth Avenue, New York, NY 10036.

TAKING ACTION
Keep your eyes peeled for outdoor concerts.

In the summer season (and even all year long, depending on where you live), there's always a concert or performance of some kind being offered in a park, at a beach, or in some other public venue. These opportunities abound in communities both large and small throughout the country, and are well-publicized in newspapers, flyers, on billboards, and on local TV segments that highlight upcoming events. Free concerts and other performances do not always feature unknown acts. Quite the contrary. Very often, these events feature groups and performers who are unflatteringly known as "has-beens," but who were once at the top of their game and are still well-known and instantly recognizable by the public. These events can be veritable entertainment gold mines for adults since the musical performers quite often were those who were in vogue when the adults were growing up.

TAKING ACTION
If music's your thing, then used CD and tape stores should be king.

If you're an aficionado of recorded music, you can make it a habit to search for your tunes at used CD and tape stores. Usually these stores are not at the top of the list of anyone who is searching for music (probably because they're not conveniently located at the mall), but these independent retailers are well worth the extra trip. One of my employees told me recently that he patronized only used CD, tape, and record stores when he was in the service, out of deference to making his paycheck go as far as possible. He went on to tell me that he built a music library consisting of hundreds of tapes and albums—the vast majority of which he still has today. The "used" option is especially conducive to consumers of CDs because their physical condition and audio quality does not substantially change over time.

TAKING ACTION

Check out the local college campus for great entertainment.

No, I'm not talking about watching fraternity brothers play pranks on their sorority counterparts or vice versa. Both large and small universities all over the country sponsor events on campus all year long. Although brought to the college for the benefit of the student body, faculty, and other associates connected with the school, they are almost always open to the public. The events and presentations that can be found on a college campus reflect the diversity that most colleges embrace. Whether your interest is plays, concerts, lectures, movies, or artistic displays invariably you'll find something that will pique your interest on the campus of a university. Frequently the events that are open to the public are well-publicized in local media outlets. A call to the school's office of cultural affairs or other similarly titled department will also yield a schedule of coming events for your benefit. The cost of such on-campus entertainment can vary, starting with free. Whatever the cost, you can be certain that you'd pay a lot more if you were to catch it elsewhere.

TAKING ACTION
Check out the sites
that made this country great.

One interesting and less expensive option you have available for entertainment is visiting historical houses, locations, and landmarks. Typically these trips end up being far more interesting than anyone thinks they will be at the outset. Many landmarks have great historical significance and really interesting stories associated with them. Depending on where you live, you might have a wealth of them in your own backyard. One of my employees grew up in the area of Lexington and Concord, Massachusetts—centerpiece towns of the American Revolutionary War. He told me that by the time he left, after having lived there roughly 20 years, he *still* hadn't seen everything there was to see. Now, you may not have as many historical sites at your fingertips, but there's more than you think. What's more, the cost of admission to these places is usually very low—often free! For more information, I suggest you contact the local tourism board in your area.

TAKING ACTION
Check out a local factory.

I can remember that some of the most interesting places I ever visited as a kid were factories. I never thought so *before* I went on the tour, but after I arrived I sure did. It can be a lot of fun to watch how certain products (even some pretty mundane ones) are made. If you have access to factories that make products such as candy, you'll find it *very* interesting. Factory tours are generally free of charge because companies like it when the public takes an interest in what they do. You may want to contact the local tourism bureau first to see which, if any, factories are on their list of available tours.

TAKING ACTION

Are you the outdoors type?
Call the Girl Scouts to save money on
camping equipment.

Camping can be a lot of fun, but getting the equipment necessary can be cost-prohibitive for some people. If it is for you, I have a possible solution: Let the Girl Scouts come to your rescue.

That's right. The Girl Scouts have a policy that if equipment gets old or becomes unwanted, it is sold at prices that are obscenely low. The going rate for used camping gear available from the Girl Scouts is roughly 75% below that which is charged in retail outlets. For more information, contact the local troops in your vicinity.

TAKING ACTION

Find a reliable source of information
about entertainment activities.

In Dallas, Texas, the *Dallas Morning News* has a special section on Fridays dedicated to what is going on in town. There is even a section that lists free activities. Another section is dedicated to kids' activities, and so on. By using this section of the newspaper, we can make our weekend plans on Friday. Of course, this also gives us enough time to look for coupons and discounts to make the weekend even more enjoyable and less costly.

Be on the lookout for other sources of information on local events. There may be local newspapers or newsletters that will fill you in on entertainment opportunities. Additionally, once you find you are interested in attending certain types of events, why not ask to be put on the respective groups' lists? For example, my family has greatly enjoyed a local marionette theater. Now we get regular mailings about upcoming shows and activities.

Having fun does not take money. I remember growing up in Chicago and watching model airplanes being flown at a public park, playing a game of pick-up basketball, and watching free fireworks displays at a local park. You and your family will share precious memories of your time together doing these special activities. You will also pass on a legacy of good times and good consumerism to your kids.

Keeping Your Shirt in the Loan Market

U nless you're independently wealthy, chances are pretty good that at some time in your life you're going to need to do some borrowing. In fact, it's likely that you have had to borrow already. If you "own" a home, you probably carry a mortgage which means you borrowed money to buy your residence in the first place. If you own a car and you are like most of us, you borrowed to purchase it. If you use credit cards, you're borrowing all the time (although many credit card companies try to make you forget that you are borrowing). Borrowing is one of those evil necessities of life. It's something to avoid as much as possible, although there really isn't much choice if you want to make major purchases such as a house.

What makes borrowing especially distasteful for many people is that it costs so much. Annual percentage rates (APRs) on different types of loans can run as high as 24% per year. Another problem with borrowing is the ease with which it now may be done. It seems as though everyone has credit cards these days, and few among us are shy about using them.

The purpose of this chapter is to help you see the forest for the trees when it comes time to borrow. Given that borrowing is such an intrinsic part of consumer life in America, it won't serve much purpose to rage on about its evils. I will remind you, however, that the Bible teaches in Proverbs 22:7: "The borrower is servant to the lender." Careful thought should be put into how to borrow wisely—and even into the possibility that you should *not* borrow in some cases. If you do decide to take out a loan check out my website at www.parislending.com.

TAKING ACTION
Before applying for any loan, run a credit check on yourself.

Whenever you apply for a loan, the lender will want to know what your credit history is before he makes his decision. Your credit history is a record of your loan obligations and a record of your payment (or repayment) history. Using this credit record, a prospective lender makes a judgment as to your *credit worthiness.* Not only will he use the document to decide whether or not to lend you money, he will also use it to decide how much interest to charge. A borrower with a poor credit history is considered a greater risk, so that person will be charged a higher interest rate by the lender (his reward for assuming the greater risk by lending the money in the first place). Obtaining the lowest interest possible should always be a priority for anyone seeking to borrow money. It becomes even more important if the person seeking to borrow doesn't have much to begin with. Therefore, it is incumbent on the prospective borrower to run a credit check on himself *before* any lenders have the opportunity to review his credit record. This way any problems can be cleared up before actually applying for the loan.

There are a number of organizations in existence that make it their business to keep track of the credit histories of the American citizenry. These organizations are called credit bureaus. They maintain files on each member of the consuming public. These files contain information, both good and bad, on the credit-related behaviors of consumers. Before you apply for a loan, you'll want to be certain that you've already seen a copy of your own credit history before the lender does. By doing so, you'll save yourself a lot of anxiety and even an application fee here and there.

There are three main credit bureaus in this country: Equifax, Experian, and Trans Union. You can never be sure which credit bureau(s) a particular lender may subscribe to, so it's a good idea to check your credit record with all three. The charge is roughly $10 apiece for each report you want sent. There is one exception which enables you to get your credit report for free from all three bureaus. Under federal law, if you are turned down for credit because of information provided by a credit bureau you are entitled to receive that agency's file on you for free.

Here are the addresses and phone numbers of the credit bureaus:

Experian
P.O. Box 2104
Allen, TX 75013
888-397-3742
www.experian.com

Equifax Information Services
P.O. Box 740241
Atlanta, GA 30374-0241
800-685-1111
www.equifax.com

Trans Union
555 West Adams
Chicago, IL 60661
312-258-1717
www.tuc.com

If you have blemishes on your credit record, fix them on your own.

Many people afflicted with a substandard credit report are under either one of two impressions: Nothing can be done to fix a sad-looking credit report, or they must pay someone a lot of money to fix it. The fact is, neither assumption is correct. If you notice some problems on your credit report that you would like to clear up, you can pay someone to handle that task for you. There are a lot of so-called "credit repair" services and clinics that would be happy to help you clean up your report . . . for a princely sum. But *you* can get your credit report looking cleaner than ever, and you don't have to pay anyone a dime to do it.

The key to making changes on your credit report lies in the wording of the Fair Credit Reporting Act. It says that information on your report may remain there for up to 7 years (10 years for bankruptcies). Notice that it doesn't say that the information *must* be present for *at least* 7 years. This seemingly minor variation in verbiage opens the door for you to use reasonable means to clean up your credit report. Now that we've determined that it's possible to make changes, do you still wonder if you would be better off to have a so-called expert do the work for you? After all, isn't your credit record too important for you to try to clean up yourself?

Nonsense. That's what credit repair outfits want you to believe. The people who do it for a living don't want you to know how easy it is—but I'll be happy to tell you. The truth is, anyone can repair his own credit. First of all, the credit bureau is obligated to immediately drop any entry from your report if the entry is inaccurate.

To dispute an inaccurate entry on your credit report—

Date

Your Name
Street Address
City, State, Zip

Name of Credit Bureau
Street Address
City, State, Zip

To: Customer Service Dept.

I have reviewed a copy of my credit file as it is maintained by your organization. To my surprise and dismay, I have discovered that some of the information contained therein is inaccurate. The purpose of this letter is to ask you to initiate an investigation immediately regarding this inaccurate information. The inaccurate entries are as follows:

> *List the name of the creditor who is the source of the entry.*
> *List the creditor code here.*
> *List the account number here.*
> *Describe the inaccuracy here.*

In accordance with the provisions of the Fair Credit Reporting Act, I expect to be advised of the results of this investigation within 30 days. Furthermore, in accordance with the Fair Credit Reporting Act, I expect that the information will be removed if it cannot be verified. Once your investigation is finished, please send me an updated copy of my credit report.

Thank you for your assistance in this matter.

Sincerely,

Your signature
Your typed name
Your Social Security number
Your date of birth

To dispute an accurate but negative entry—

Date

Your Name
Street Address
City, State, Zip

Name of Credit Bureau
Street Address
City, State, Zip

To: Customer Service Dept.

I have reviewed a copy of my credit file as it is maintained by your organization. My copy of this credit file contains the following entries which I would like to have reverified at once.

> *List the name of the creditor who is the source of the entry.*
> *List the creditor code here.*
> *List the account number here.*

In accordance with the Fair Credit Reporting Act, I expect to be advised of the results of this investigation within 30 days. Furthermore, in accordance with the Fair Credit Reporting Act, I expect that the information will be removed if it cannot be reverified. Once your investigation is finished, please send me an updated copy of my credit report.

Thank you for your assistance in this matter.

Sincerely,

Your signature
Your typed name
Your Social Security number
Your date of birth

You certainly don't need any third party to help you get that done. Simply write a letter to the credit bureau describing the inaccuracy, and they'll take it up with the creditor or collection agency who put it on there in the first place. (A sample letter expressly designed for this kind of situation is found on page 183.)

What may not be as apparent, however, is that you can even remove information from your credit report which is negative but accurate by using the "dispute" method. The dispute method allows you to take advantage of the phraseology found in part in the Fair Credit Reporting Act by letting you ask the credit bureaus to reverify any part of your report you want. The dispute method is the only industry-accepted method of cleaning up a credit report.

To dispute an entry on your credit report, you need to write a letter to the *credit bureau*, not to the creditor listed as being the source of the entry. The bureau has 30 days to check out your grievance with the original creditor. If the creditor doesn't respond to the bureau quickly enough, the bureau is obligated to drop the information from your report. Unfortunately, it's also possible that the original creditor *will* respond to the credit bureau, verifying that the entry is indeed accurate and should remain on your report. If that happens, wait a little while and dispute the item again. Remember, you're within your rights to dispute these items; you don't have to sit idly by and let entries that reflect negatively on your credit record remain there unchallenged. For the best chance of success, though, you must be willing to follow a few simple rules regarding your credit-repair efforts.

First of all, always dispute with the credit bureau, *not* with the creditor. The reason for this is that it's the bureau that must abide by the 30-day rule, so there's a greater likelihood of success if you channel your efforts through them. Second, be careful to word your dispute letter properly. I've included two sample letters you may use in your dispute efforts. The first one is designed to help you remove information that is totally inaccurate, while the second one is written to help you delete entries that may be factually correct but reflect badly on your record.

TAKING ACTION
Consider tapping the equity in your home.

If you need to borrow some money, you may want to consider using the equity of your home to do it. The advantages of a home equity loan are significant. First of all, approval is usually very easy and simple because you're putting up something of tremendous value as collateral. Another advantage is that the approval process, often a source of headaches for prospective borrowers, is no big deal in acquiring home equity loans. Also, the home equity loan business has become so popular in recent years that it's not difficult to find banks which will waive the closing costs completely, thereby decreasing the overall cost of your loan. Another plus to home equity loans is that they're available so readily these days. This means you should be able to secure a great rate simply by shopping around. Finally, the interest charged on a home equity loan is almost always tax-deductible, which enhances their viability as a borrowing mechanism even further.

While we're discussing this, let's dispel the common misconception that home equity loans must be used for home-improvement purposes. Home equity loans can be used for anything; they're not required to be used for repairs, additions, or other expenses related directly or indirectly to the home.

I know of one person, for example, who needed to buy a car fast but was hard up for money. Instead of applying for a standard auto loan, he simply tapped the equity in his home. Now he's deducting the interest he's paying, something he would not be able to do if he had chosen to obtain a traditional auto loan.

I don't want to pretend that home equity loans represent nothing but sunshine and laughter. If you get behind on the loan, remember that you could lose your home since it's pledged as collateral. Nonetheless, as long as you are able to remain cognizant of that very important detail, it's wise to keep the option of the home equity loan in mind if you need to do some quick borrowing. The rates you'll find available should be the most competitive of any for which you'll qualify.

TAKING ACTION
Consider borrowing from your retirement plan.

One of the keys to borrowing for less lies in your ability to find money sources beyond banks and other typically considered types of lenders. A great alternative for those people who have 401(k) plans at work is to borrow from *them*. When you borrow from your 401(k), you don't face the same application and administrative fees that you do when you borrow from a lending institution—and the interest rate you'll receive is lower than that charged by those same lenders. What's also nice is that when you borrow from your retirement plan, you're borrowing from yourself, so what you pay back goes into your own account. This is a terrific loan option for people without a lot of money.

Do remember, however, that you're borrowing from your retirement plan—the very money source which will one day keep you warm and cozy at night. I suggest maintaining the same amount of enthusiasm toward repaying the money as you have about tapping the fund in the first place. Also know that if you leave your job before the loan is repaid, you have to repay it in full at that time or it will be regarded as a withdrawal and you'll face some IRS music.

You'll notice that I did not include the option of borrowing from an IRA or Keogh retirement plan in my discussion of this principle. The reason is that you may only borrow from them for a period of up to 60 days. While this may be of some assistance in a short-term need situation, the reality is that 60 days is not usually long enough to permit you to regard the money as a real loan.

TAKING ACTION

Whenever possible, opt for a home equity line of credit instead of a second mortgage.

In my experience as a financial counselor, I find that when the subject of borrowing against the equity in one's home comes up, many people use the terms "home equity line of credit" and "second mortgage" interchangeably. They are not one and the same. With a home equity loan, you receive a *line of credit* against the equity in your home. When you borrow against the equity, you pay interest only on what you've borrowed. With a second mortgage, you receive a lump sum against the equity in your home. You must pay interest on the whole amount whether you use the money in its entirety or not. Now, if the reason you're borrowing in the first place is because you need a substantial sum of money right away, it probably doesn't matter whether you choose the home equity loan or the second mortgage. However, if you anticipate that you'll need to use the money for a variety of purposes over a longer period of time, better to tap it when you need it so that you save yourself a lot of money in interest charges.

TAKING ACTION
Do not accept a home equity loan card if offered.

The latest gimmick to be propagated by those seeking your home equity business is something called a home equity loan card. A home equity loan card is like any other credit card, except that instead of the money being withdrawn against an unsecured line of credit, it's being drawn against your home. The chief advantage espoused by those advising you to take this card is that it is a lot easier for you to tap into your line of credit. However, always assume that if a lending institution claims to want to make life easier on you, then it's likely that you will pay a higher price down the line for that ease and simplicity. So it is with home equity cards. When the lender allows you to access your line of credit in the form of a credit card, he will almost always demand that you pay a higher rate of interest to do so. This means that a home equity loan which can be had for, say, 8% when accessed by more traditional means, can cost as much as some high-interest credit cards when accessed in the form of a credit card. The other problem with home equity cards is that they encourage reckless spending. A home equity loan should be taken out only for important, major, or otherwise well-thought-out purchases. If you carry your home equity loan credit card in your wallet, however, there's more of a chance that you may decide to use it for incidental purchases.

Remember, your home is at stake when you take out a home equity loan. For someone without much money, the home equity loan can be a nice alternative to some of the other borrowing mechanisms which charge a lot more in interest. However, as with any borrowing tool, the home equity option should be used very wisely.

TAKING ACTION

Consider tapping the cash value in your whole life policy for a low-interest loan.

If you have read any of my previous books, you know that I'm not a big fan of whole life, or cash-value, life insurance. I simply believe that the policies are much too expensive for the supposed perks they offer beyond the death benefit. However, if you already have a whole life policy, it wouldn't hurt to look to it in the event you need a loan. If you have had the policy long enough to have built up some measure of cash value, you can borrow from it at very nice terms. The interest rates are usually very low (most of which is actually paid back to your own account), and you can take as long as you want to repay the money. Those are excellent terms as far as borrowing goes. Remember, though, that whenever you borrow from your policy, the death benefit will be diminished by the outstanding amount if the in-sured dies before the money's repaid.

Credit Cards

Credit card use and possession is worthy of a special section. Credit cards are still used much more than they should be. They represent a "double whammy" for so many who have so little, be-cause they are too easy to use, and they hit the cardholder with exorbitant costs when he or she uses them.

TAKING ACTION
If you need a loan, look to your credit card last.

The fastest, easiest loans you'll ever get are the lines of credit represented by your credit cards. For some people, the borrow-ing power can be substantial. Many people have individual card limits of $5,000 or more, meaning that they can borrow as much as $10,000 to $25,000 with very little effort. Unfortunately, some of the worst deals in lending are found at the offices of the issuers of the credit cards in your wallet.

Many people who carry around credit cards with finance charges of around 20 percent per year could probably qualify for a bank loan of some sort with interest closer to the prime rate (the Prime Rate is an oft-used benchmark by lenders, defined as the interest rate that banks charge their most credit-worthy corporate customers to borrow). Most credit card issuers make you pay dearly for the privilege of accessing a line of credit so easily.

The other problem with looking to your credit cards as a source of loan funds is that your cards should be used only in emergencies (you should only have two or three cards—see "Financial Freedom on a Budget," pp. 23-24). If you load up your cards with a lot of charges that could have been financed elsewhere, you are depriving yourself of the full use of those cards if and when you get into a real jam.

Keep away from credit cards and stick to the more traditional loan routes when it's time to borrow.

Credit cards should not be your first borrowing resource unless you have very specific reasons why you are using them ahead of home equity loans and the like. Nonetheless, their ease of access and use means that they will continue to be tapped by some people looking for no-hassle loans. If you do insist on using them from time to time, do so with the utmost level of prudence.

TAKING ACTION

Cancel credit cards that don't offer grace periods.

Any credit card worth its salt will offer a grace period to its cardholders. The grace period is that portion of time between when you make a designated purchase and when you are charged interest on that same purchase. A card with a 25-day grace period is very typical. Always avoid the cards which charge interest on your purchases starting from the moment you make them. For people who don't have a lot of money, cards without grace periods should be avoided entirely.

TAKING ACTION
Use your credit card to borrow interest-free from the bank.

What I'm talking about is something you may have heard mentioned before; float. Float is the time which elapses between your purchase and the date the purchase is actually debited from your account. The amount of time you have between bills is usually about 20 days, and if the merchant drags his feet in submitting your particular bill, you can have a lot longer to enjoy the float time. In general, you have about 30 days whenever you make a purchase with a credit card to pay for it without incurring any interest charges. For this 30-day period, your money can be sitting in some kind of interest-bearing account.

Thus, not only will you get to put off paying the bill for about a month, you will actually earn additional money on those funds. Again, though, this distinct advantage of being able to borrow for free for up to 30 days (and even make money on the deal) only works if you are diligent about paying off your purchases in full before the interest charges are assessed. For someone who doesn't have much money, this strategic method of using credit cards can be an especially good deal.

TAKING ACTION
Consider carrying a credit card that rewards you for using it.

One of the latest trends in the credit card world is the one that offers rebates on goods and services purchased on the card—if it matches or exceeds a certain dollar amount each year. For example, auto manufacturers and telephone companies are issuing their own MasterCards and Visas these days, promising to reward you with rebates if you use their cards to rack up a certain dollar amount of purchases. These cards can be good deals if you are confident that you will want or use the benefits they offer. I am aware, for example, of a supermarket chain by the name of Kroger that has its own MasterCard (issued in conjunction with US Bank) that gives cardholders a rebate on total annual purchases made at Kroger. Now, I'm not all of a sudden saying that I think credit cards are the way to go and that you should use these particular kinds of cards willy-nilly. All I'm saying is that if you are going to use a credit card at all, you should know that these opportunities exist. (Check out other credit cards at www.credit-land.com.) Either way, always strive to pay off your balance each month. You're not obligated to keep a balance with these cards and pay interest to receive the bonuses.

TAKING ACTION

Be wary of using your credit card for cash advances.

If you use your credit card at an ATM machine to get cash regularly, it's no wonder that your cash flow is tight. If you thought ATM fees were bad when you used your standard bank ATM card, you haven't seen anything until you use your credit card to make a withdrawal. When you use your regular ATM card at an ATM machine owned by an entity other than your own bank, the fees can be high—up to $4 in some cases. However, when you use your credit card the fees can close in on the $10 mark. Furthermore, in many cases, the interest rate charged by your card issuer on cash advances can be a lot higher than what they charge on regular purchases. Between the advance fees and the higher interest rate, using a credit card for the purpose of getting money out of an ATM is not what anyone short on cash should be doing.

TAKING ACTION
Resist purchasing credit life and/or disability insurance with your loans.

Whenever you apply for a loan from a bank or other lending institution, it's very likely that you will get a sales pitch on credit life and disability insurance. The purpose of these coverages is to ensure than your loan obligation will be repaid in the event you die or become disabled and cannot work. However if you are having a difficult time keeping money in your hands right now, you should certainly cancel these coverages if you have them. First of all, they are generally overpriced. Furthermore, they probably duplicate coverages you already have (at least the credit life should). In other words, instead of purchasing an array of different life insurance policies on behalf of each of your loan obligations, you should have one inexpensive term life insurance policy which covers *all* your obligations. If you haven't purchased any of these merchant-sold coverages at this point, let this serve as fair warning that it's something you don't want to do.

TAKING ACTION

Do not purchase extended warranties.

When you purchase a consumer good of some kind, there's a good chance that you'll have the opportunity to purchase an extended warranty to go along with it. Before you go out and purchase your next piece of electronics equipment, an appliance, or anything else for which an extended warranty may be sold, decide *before* you get to the store that you're not going to pay for the extended warranty—no matter how good the deal may sound coming from the salesperson's lips. Extended warranties sound great at first, but anyone who has purchased one will tell you that they are little more than profit centers for the retail stores selling them. Here's why.

Extended warranties are very expensive for what they are. In general, less than 20% (in some cases a lot less) of the money collected on extended warranty purchases is used to pay for repairs; the remainder is profit. This brings me to the next problem with these plans. The salespeople who push these things are normally compensated with huge commissions if they successfully sell them. This is where most of the rest of the money goes. Beyond all this, extended warranties are usually pretty restrictive in that they don't cover what mostly goes awry with the merchandise you've purchased. Finally, experts will tell you that if something fundamental is going to go wrong with your purchase, it will likely go wrong during the first year you own it—while it's still covered by the manufacturer's warranty. Statistics show that if the product makes it to the end of the first year without a problem, it will likely continue to operate without incident until normal wear and tear (which is *not* covered by an extended war-ranty) brings its life to an end.

TAKING ACTION
Consider repaying loans with bank debits.

One of the quickest ways to drain your bank account unneces-sarily each month is to pay your obligations late and face the associ-ated fees and other assessments from your creditors. If you pay your mortgage after a certain due date each month, for example, you must pay an additional sum of money on top of the regular amount due as a late fee. The same goes with your car payment. Many other credi-tors also make late fees part of the terms of your contract with them. The surest way around getting stuck with these charges on a regular basis is to take advantage of any opportunities which come your way to pay your obligations with the now-common bank debit mechanism.

Frequently, your creditors will give you a chance to arrange to pay your obligations by having your bank account automatically deb-ited. Although there is reluctance on the part of some people to allow "outsiders" access to their bank accounts, there are a great many checks and balances in place. These make it well-nigh impossible for an unscrupulous creditor or creditor employee to take advantage of you through your bank account(s). The advantages of paying your bills this way are obvious. Any tendencies toward procrastination you have when it comes to bill-paying are short-circuited. Furthermore, as a secondary benefit, you will save money because you won't be us-ing checks or stamps to pay these obligations (that doesn't sound like a major benefit, but if you truly have very little money you know that every little bit helps).

Whenever you seek a loan, be sure to check out your options at a number of different institutions.

In the first principle I mentioned in this chapter, I spoke about how important it was to ensure that your credit record looked as sharp as possible. Although this can be important for a number of reasons it is critical when it comes to your efforts to obtain a loan for the lowest rate of interest possible. However, taking steps to clean up your credit report before you approach lenders is only half of the battle. The other half is making certain that you "shop out" that credit record to as many lenders as you can before you settle on an offer from one of them.

Take an auto loan, for example. Applying for an auto loan should cost you nothing, so you can feel comfortable applying for the loan through as many lenders as you want. Many lenders will take loan applications over the telephone, thus the process is relatively hassle-free and takes only a few minutes. You may be surprised at the wide variance in rates offered by the different lenders you approach—and you'll find this to be true for virtually any kind of loan you pursue.

Shopping around is perhaps the most valuable, most under-used strategy there is in consumerism. Don't be shy about contacting a number of prospective lenders; making loans is how banks make the vast majority of their money. By looking at several lenders you put yourself in the driver's seat, which is how it should be.

TAKING ACTION

Avoid adjustable rate mortgages whenever possible.

Let me say right off the bat that adjustable rate mortgages (ARMs) have their place. If you want to purchase a home but know in advance that you won't be in it for more than a few years, an adjustable rate mortgage may be the way to go. Adjustable rate mortgages typically offer borrowers the opportunity to borrow at lower than the prevailing fixed rates for the first few years of the loan. The payoff to the lender comes afterward in the form of rising rates. However, if you're going to be in your house for only a few years, it's likely that you will be out of the house (as well as the mortgage) before the mortgage rate has a chance to go up.

That's but one example of a few specialized situations that make adjustable rate mortgages smart choices. However, adjustable rate mortgages are not good choices for most people because they cost more in the long run. Even though most ARMs "cap out" at a certain point, it's more than probable that you'll pay a lot more for the privilege of borrowing. Therefore opt for a fixed-rate mortgage if you're in the market for a home. Not only will you pay less over the long haul, your costs will be much more predictable. With the ARM, you can't be certain from year to year what your monthly mortgage payment will be. With the fixed rate mortgage, you will know exactly what your mortgage payment is going to be now and in the future. This is important for people who are perpetually short on cash because it makes dealing with the monthly budget and making spending plans for the future a whole lot easier.

TAKING ACTION

If you currently have an ARM, take steps to see if you're being overcharged.

One of the problems with adjustable rate mortgages is that they are complicated in structure. That makes it a lot easier for lenders to incorrectly calculate the payments due. Some mortgage experts claim that over 50% of all adjustable rate mortgage payments have been miscalculated. *Over 50%!* Obviously, if you're short of money and currently have an adjustable rate mortgage, it may be to your advantage to determine if you're getting overcharged by your lender. There are companies that will review your mortgage to see if you're being charged correctly. Unfortunately, it costs to have the review done, which isn't the best of news. However, even if you cannot get the review done soon, you may be able to afford it after you've allowed time for some of these other principle suggestions to bear fruit.

The cost to have your mortgage checked should be about $100. But consider the tremendous upside potential of having this done—you could save thousands of dollars over the life of your loan. To give you a head start, there is a company in Maryland, Loantechs, that will review your mortgage and issue a written report for $95. You can reach Loantech at 800-888-6781.

TAKING ACTION

To keep your mortgage rate down, go to a wholesaler.

In this day and age of consumerism, we're all finding that new, low-cost versions of old full-service retail services are popping up everywhere. Some life insurance companies have cut out using agents in the field, lowering the cost of the policies and passing the savings on to their consumers. In the investment industry, no-load mutual funds and discount brokers are the order of the day. Now we're starting to see this trend toward cutting out the middleman come to the lending industry. What I'm talking about is the wholesaling of mortgages.

Keep your eyes peeled for wholesalers. By getting rid of middlemen, these folks have been able to successfully offer mortgages which are noticeably lower than the prevailing rates. You can find mortgage sources at my website: www. parislending.com.

TAKING ACTION

Beware of industry recommendations when deciding how much to borrow.

It is a generally-accepted notion in the real-estate business that when determining how much house you can afford, you are "allowed" to allocate up to 29% of your gross monthly income toward your mortgage payment. A lot of eager home-buyers seize on that figure and go out and buy a house that means they must spend that much (or more) on their mortgage payment.

They think, *It may seem like a lot to some people, but hey, if the industry-types say it's okay, then it's okay, right?*

What a minute. Doesn't it seem a little suspicious that it's the *mortgage and real-estate* industry that came up with that guideline? Doesn't that strike you as being a little self-serving? According to that "rule," a family grossing $30,000 per year (or $2,500 per month) can spend as much as $725 per month on their monthly mortgage payment. That's a lot of money, considering that it's based on *gross* income and that you'll have a lot of other expenses to think about each month.

Don't listen to what an industry says you *should* spend on their products or services. (The diamond industry, for example, says you should spend two months' salary on an engagement ring. This means that a person making only $12,000 per year should buy a $2,000 engagement ring!) Each industry has a vested interest in seeing that you spend as much as possible in their respective areas of commerce. Spend what seems comfortable—and practical—to you. Before you settle on any loan offer, know exactly what your monthly payments will be. Rework your budget *on paper* to see how much you will be impacted by the new arrangement *before* you settle on it. If things seem a little tight, then you probably need to make a readjustment of some kind.

TAKING ACTION

Highly disciplined families should strive to set up their own finance fund.

This is a great idea for people who don't have immediate borrowing needs but would like an excellent alternative to paying outrageous finance charges in the future when they *do* need to borrow.

With the finance fund, you make regular deposits into a cash reserve account (like a money-market fund paying a competitive rate of interest). Then, when the fund has reached a sufficient size, a member of the family who needs to borrow can do so from the family finance fund—with the twist that he will pay back the fund with interest (to ensure its continued existence), in the same fashion that he would repay a loan from a bank or other lending institution. What's nice about this is there aren't other fees to be paid or bankers to deal with. You can establish an interest rate that is less than what you would be able to receive anywhere else.

The only problems with this idea are that it isn't very helpful to people who need to borrow in the near future, and only the most disciplined of families can make it work. Nonetheless, it's a great way to be able to borrow for a lot less than you would be able to from any other entity.

In closing, borrowing can be done wisely. Unfortunately the words borrow and wisely are rarely spoken in the same breath. In life, most often the truth can be found between the extremes. In the case of borrowing, I think it is utterly impractical to teach that Christians should never borrow. Biblical teaching certainly supports that a great deal of caution should be taken in this area, but in reality the case *cannot* be made that the Bible prohibits the use of debt. By the same token the case *cannot* be made that the Bible encourages the use of debt, either. On this subject, my best advice to you is to proceed carefully with your eyes wide open and with much thought and prayer. I've never met anyone who felt they borrowed too little in their lifetime. I *have* met countless thousands, however, whose broken marriages and financial insolvency serve as a testimony to the dangers and ravages of the misuse of debt.

Incredible Vacations
Anyone Can Afford

If you don't have much money, traveling is probably not one of your hobbies. Traveling may not be the unreachable star you think it is. If you're willing to take a little initiative, you'll find that there are a lot of ways to save money on traveling…including ways to take free vacations! As with anything, knowing what's out there is the key. So without further delay, let me share some knowledge that may make the difference between you and your family enjoying a quality, well-deserved respite or remaining stuck at home in front of the television, watching other people see the world. First; my website, www.christianmoney.com, has a travel section that offers deals and discounts on cruises, hotels, and airfare.

TAKING ACTION

When making
hotel reservations, call late.

It has been said that in order to realize a good deal on a room rate it's better to call individual hotels to make your reservations rather than the chain's national reservations line. That may or not be true, but one thing does seem to be for sure: Where you call to make your booking may not matter as much as when you call.

If you call to make your reservation late in the evening, chances are you'll have the reservationist's full attention. His phone won't likely be ringing off the hook, and therefore he'll have more time to go back and forth with you when discussing (negotiating?) an acceptable room rate. It has even been suggested that by calling late at night, you'll get yourself a savings of 10% or so right off the bat. Whether that applies in your case or not remains to be seen, but either way, make your reservations late at night and be certain to force the issue of discounts or breaks by asking about them right away.

TAKING ACTION
Try a hotel discount service.

Hotel discount networks are organizations that through volume arrangements with the major hotel chains have access to large discounts for their customers. In many cases these discounts can be as much as 65% of the normal rate. One such organization that I recommend is Hotels.com at 800-96-HOTEL.

TAKING ACTION
Look to weekend getaways to provide you with a short vacation.

If you're busy and find yourself constantly harried with concerns that are both home and work related, then you probably need a short vacation to recharge your batteries—that's what's so great about the weekend getaway. I find that when I take my family away for a weekend, we all seem to get the break we need. And we are able to do so without spending an arm and a leg or becoming bothered by the many other concerns we face when we take an extended vacation.

One good way to save money on weekend getaways is to stay in hotels that cater to business travelers. Typically, these hotels don't have high occupancy rates on weekends—so a lot of them will have reduced weekend prices. Some will even offer weekend "getaway" rates that are considerably lower than those found during the week. The key is to track down these business traveler hotels. For instance, if you plan on going to a theme park on your trip, stay away from the nearby hotels. Instead, look for those hotels that are located in the business district, far away from the tourist strip. You may have to drive a little farther to get where you want to be, but the money you save will make it all worthwhile. For example, in Dallas I have stayed at five-star hotels on such weekend getaways for as little as $65 per night, a hefty discount from the normal rates which can be as much as $200.

TAKING ACTION
Avoid making telephone calls from your hotel room.

There can be a wide disparity among hotels with respect to their policies regarding in-room telephone use. It is not at all uncommon for hotels to charge outrageous usage fees, even for local calls. My advice? Find out the complete cost of phone usage from your room at check-in. If it is unreasonable, use the pay phone in the lobby to make your calls. Remember, some hotels will charge you even if you make calls with a credit card, so know the score *before* you pick up the receiver.

TAKING ACTION
Don't go on vacation to watch movies.

Many hotels and motels offer cable television, including at least one or two "premium" channels, as part of the regular room rate. Additionally, many will make pay-for-view movies available in the room as well. The pay-movie options can be tempting because the movies are usually first-run films. However, these films can be expensive. Be careful. It is sometimes too easy to buy the film and pay for it; if you hit a wrong button on the in-room TV remote, you pay for the movie.

Why are you taking a vacation in the first place . . . to go to the movies? Not likely. It can be tempting to hit a button and watch a popular first-run movie, but remember how expensive a proposition it can be.

TAKING ACTION
Skip the room service.

Ah, room service. Nothing serves as a finer representation of true vacation living than having someone prepare your meals and deliver them right to your room. As will all such perks, however, this one can cost big. Generally, the meals are more expensive, and once you factor in the tip to the waiter who delivers the meal, you can easily find yourself paying substantially more than you need to for breakfast, lunch, or dinner. Accessing room service can be tempting, especially after a full day of sightseeing or shopping. My suggestion is that you tough it out and drag yourself downstairs to the dining room or another eatery outside the hotel.

TAKING ACTION
See a copy of your bill each day of your stay.

Another good way to ensure that you keep your vacation spending in check is to review a copy of your bill each day. Each morning, head to the front desk and ask the clerk to print out a copy of your bill as it stands currently. By checking your bill closely, you can keep track of all the entries and be certain that you're not letting your hotel expenses get out of control.

TAKING ACTION
Remember the occupancy tax.

If you stay in hotels or motels with any regularity, you've probably noticed that the amount you pay for your room is noticeably more expensive than the rate you're quoted at check-in or when you make your reservation. The reason for this is the occupancy tax (also known as the bed tax or room tax). The occupancy tax in some cities can be high, as much as 20% or more. It's a stiff addition to the rate you're paying. There's really nothing you can do to avoid paying the occupancy tax, but you should at least know what your total room rate is going to be when you're shopping around. When you ask for a quote on a room, make sure to ask for a quote that includes the occupancy tax.

TAKING ACTION
Be certain to remember
your discount-earning memberships.

I find that many people do not take advantage of the travel and entertainment benefits offered by their memberships in various organizations nearly as often as they should. There are copious numbers of membership-based groups that offer breaks on hotel rates, rental car rates, and a number of other travel-related expenses. One of my employees was telling me recently that his annual membership fee for AAA always pays for itself because of all the travel-related discounts he realizes from it. If you belong to an organization of any kind that has as its benefits the opportunity to save on travel-related services, by all means use them.

TAKING ACTION
When renting a car, go for utility.

Whenever you run across an ad for a car rental company on television, you always see a shiny, new, slick-looking vehicle shown as the representation of what you can drive if you come to them with your business. If, however, you are seeking travel transportation on a limited budget, consider the agencies that specialize in renting "very used" cars. Known by names such as "Rent-a-Wreck" and "Ugly Duckling," these companies provide functional, well-maintained vehicles for half, if not less, of the price of renting a newer car from one of the better-known agencies. Believe me, no discount you have for Hertz, Avis, or any of the other biggies in the car rental industry will compare to the savings you'll realize by renting from a company that only rents older used cars.

Because these agencies don't usually advertise very prominently, you'll have to hunt them out on your own. The best place to go is the Yellow Pages, under the heading "Automobile Renting and Leasing." You'll find at least a couple of options for used car renting. If you will fly to the destination where you'll rent your car, scout the rental agency that you'll be using ahead of time—especially since most of these used-car rental locations are not convenient to tourist areas. You may have to take a cab from the airport to the agency, but even paying the cab fare to and from the used car rental agency will do little to limit the savings you'll realize from going with this option in the first place.

If you plan on renting the car for a long road trip, check the car out thoroughly beforehand. Although these cars are generally well-maintained, they're not really intended to be used by folks who plan on driving hundreds of miles each day for several days in a row. In fact, these agencies came into being to fill the needs of local residents who needed cars for utilitarian purposes but didn't want to pay the high rates of the more glamorous, tourist-based agencies.

TAKING ACTION

Rent your car at an agency site far away from the airport.

Whether you decide to rent a very used car or one like those that fly by you on the TV commercials, you would do well to transact your business at an agency site that is far removed from the airport. The majority of rental business is done at locations either at the airport or within a few miles of it. There are, however, rental locations all over in cities and towns across America. You'll find that the rental rates of agencies located a good distance from airports are often lower than those near the airports because their cars are in less demand. Saving an additional 10% to 20% off the rental price of your car is not uncommon by going this route.

TAKING ACTION

Whenever possible, rent your car as a corporate customer.

When you rent a car, do so as a corporate customer. It is no secret that rental rates, like hotel room rates, are usually much lower for corporate customers. If there is any way you can claim corporate status when renting a car, do it. You can save 20% or more in price.

TAKING ACTION
Decline the rental agency's insurance coverage.

If you rent a car, the agency representative will try to sell you the agency's version of insurance coverage on the car. I say "the agency's version" because what you are being offered is not really insurance per se. If it were, the rental car business would be, at least in part, under the auspices of the appropriate state insurance commissioners. What you are being sold are collision damage and loss damage "waivers," designed to accomplish the same thing: Indemnify you if the car is damaged or stolen.

Don't take it. Although it may sound cheap in a raw dollar sense, the coverage is really very expensive when you consider that your own auto policy probably covers you for rental cars (be sure to check, however). Plus, if you rent the car with a major credit card, additional coverage may be automatically included. It's true that if you buy the waivers then get in an accident, you can walk away from the car without paying another penny. But what are the odds of the car sustaining damage so great that your own policy isn't enough? If that's true, maybe you should stay home.

A couple of caveats. First, when you pick up the car, you will be asked to inspect it by the agent and note any damage of any kind. This is for your protection (so that the agency can't hold you responsible for preexisting damage to the car). Take the task seriously and check the car closely! Also, before you decline the waivers offered by the rental car company, be advised that your own insurance typically covers you for no more than the value of your own personal automobile. This means that if you own and have appropriate insurance coverage for a 1980 Toyota Celica, you may be in big financial trouble if you rent and subsequently damage a BMW.

TAKING ACTION
Get a detailed statement when you return the car.

When you drop off the car, ask for a detailed statement before you finish paying for the rental. It is not uncommon for a rental car customer to find additional charges (other than those clearly mentioned at the outset of the transaction) on his bill. For example, many agencies charge for additional drivers, and will also charge if they pick up or drop off the car for you at your location. Know in advance what you're being charged for; then, when you review your detailed statement at turn-in, contest any additional charges that appear.

TAKING ACTION
Consult the Entertainment coupon book for significant travel savings.

When it comes to travel and entertainment, few coupon books or offers beat those found in the Entertainment book. Entertainment Publications specializes in producing coupon books that contain significant savings for people asking to save money in their diversionary endeavors. In fact, Entertainment publishes coupon books specifically for travelers. How can you beat that? The coupon savings found in these books do not translate into just a few dollars saved here and there, either; you'll find savings of up to 50% off the regular rates for hotels found in over 100 American cities, with lots more savings available on meals and other travel-related expenses. To find out more, contact Entertainment Publications at P.O. Box 1068, Trumbull, CT 06611. You may also call them at 800-477-3234.

TAKING ACTION

If you're serious about traveling and saving, consider a discount travel service.

If you travel frequently, or would like to travel more often than you do currently, you may find serious value in becoming a member of a discount travel service. Most of these services cost between $50 and $100 per year to join, but the savings realized can be tremendous. For example, America at 50 Percent publishes a travel book that lists almost 1,500 hotels across the country where members can save 50% off of the regular (rack) room rate. Your membership could conceivably pay for itself after one night! As big as this savings is, there are additional benefits to joining America at 50 Percent, including car rental discounts and air fare rebates. You can purchase the America at 50 Percent travel book by calling Media 2 at 410-825-3463. The hotels featured through America at 50 Percent are along the lines of Holiday Inns and Best Westerns, so they're probably perfectly suitable for your purposes. However, if your tastes are a bit extravagant, you might want to consider a membership in Quest International. An annual membership costs $99, but the hotels featured are those such as Hiltons and Marriotts.

You may also want to consider a membership in Encore at $49 per year. Encore gives its members the chance to save 50% at over 4,000 hotels in the United States, Canada, and Europe. Additionally, there are tremendous savings to be had through Encore when you rent cars, dine out, and make airline reservations as a member. To find out more, give Encore a call at 301-459-8020. Consider these other money saving organizations:

The Cruise Travel Club	800-685-6518
The International Air Travel Club	800-576-2242
Domestic Air Travel Club	800-576-2999

These three travel clubs are all affiliated with *Best Fares* magazine and are free to subscribers to this publication. It is well worth the money. *Best Fares* magazine can be reached at 800-576-1234 or www.bestfares.com.

TAKING ACTION

Give yourself a dream vacation in Mexico.

One of the little-known secrets of traveling in Mexico is that you can save a fortune off of the cost of a vacation residence, compared to what a similar residence would go for here in this country. For example, if you were to rent a beachfront villa in the States for a week, you would likely pay $500 to $1,000 or more. In Mexico, however, you can rent such a residence for as little as a few hundred dollars a month—and usually maid service and utilities are included!

In recent times, the best bargains in Mexico can be found in Guadalajara, but you'll save big no matter where you go. Call a travel agent who has knowledge of the Mexican market for more information.

TAKING ACTION
House swap, and stay at your vacation destination for free!

If you don't have a problem with the idea of another family living in your house, you might find that house swapping can go a long way to giving you a very inexpensive vacation. Most people to whom I speak about this option always react with, "What a great idea! Why didn't I think of that?" The truth is, house swapping can be a great deal for everyone involved.

One of the concerns raised about house swapping is from people who don't live in a stereotypical tourist location. They balk at the idea, believing that no one will be interested in staying where their house is located. Don't be too sure. People travel to all parts of the country for a wide variety of reasons. Someone may want to come to your little "neck of the woods" because they have relatives in the area or for some reason you might not even begin to consider. What I'm saying is, if you're in the position where you know that house swapping will enable you to potentially take vacations that you otherwise wouldn't be able to afford, don't decide against pursuing this option because of a preconceived notion you have about the desirability (or lack thereof) of your home's location.

House swapping is accomplished by way of membership in clubs or subscriptions to publications that are joined by or subscribed to by other prospective swappers. One of the most widely circulated exchange publications is published by Vacation Exchange Club (P.O. Box 650, Key West, FL 33041, 800-638-3841). For $60 per year, you receive an annual directory that includes your home's listing, plus monthly updates. Current circulation is 16,000 members worldwide.

One note. Be certain that your homeowner's policy will cover you when renting out your home or using it to house nonfamily members. If you're not certain, contact your insurance company. If you guess and guess incorrectly, you may have to pay out-of-pocket for any damage done to your home by the family with whom you swap.

TAKING ACTION
When considering a cruise, always negotiate.

It seems as though everyone loves cruises. If I speak about traveling to anyone who has never been on a cruise, they all say the same thing: "I'm just dying to go on a cruise!" Cruises *are* a lot of fun, and they are extremely popular.

It is that popularity that you can use to your advantage. The chief problem with cruises for prospective travelers is the price. Cruises can be unbelievably expensive, with a trip lasting just a few days costing over $1,000. However, as the seas have become infested with cruise ships in search of a piece of the cruise business, the prices have come down. In some cases, they've come down a lot.

You can always find discounts, but sometimes the length-of-stay requirements or the tour route itself to which you must adhere to earn the discounted price may be objectionable. Is there any other way, then, to get a break on a cruise? Sure…negotiate.

Cruise ships are desperate for business...that's a fact. Therefore, you're in the driver's seat, to some extent. If you see a cruise you might like to take being advertised for a particular price, always try and get it lowered. Rarely is the list price final or not subject to negotiation. The trouble is, most consumers believe the cruise prices are another one of the many things that are carved in stone. Not true at all. If you don't like to haggle over prices, book your cruise through a travel agent. Any travel agent worth his salt will know the bottom-line prices that cruise lines will accept. However, I strongly encourage you to try to do this on your own; strive to save as much money as possible at all times.

TAKING ACTION
Use a discount airline and save up to 80%.

Although the discount airlines have been under scrutiny since the crash of a Value Jet flight in Miami, overall these airlines have not been proven to be unsafe. By flying with these lesser-known airlines you can realize incredible savings. Listed below are some of the larger discounters. Keep in mind that each has its own routes and some may not serve your part of the country. A complete list of discount airlines can be found at www.independent-traveler.com.

AirTran Airways	**American Trans Air (ATA)**
800-247-8726	800-435-9282
Hub: Atlanta	Hubs: Chicago/Midway,
	Indianapolis
America West	
800-235-9292	**Delta Express**
Hubs: Columbus,	800-325-5205
Las Vegas, Phoenix	

Frontier	**JetBlue Airline**
800-432-1359	800-538-2583
	Hubs: New York/JFK,
Gulfstream	Los Angeles, Long Beach
International Air	
800-525-0280	**Southwest**
(Florida destinations)	800-435-9792
800-231-0856	
(Bahama destinations)	**Spirit Airlines**
	800-772-7117

TAKING ACTION

Fly internationally as an air courier.

If you've ever thought of flying to an international destination for a vacation, you were likely put off immediately by the cost of the air fare. What's an international round-trip ticket cost now... $800? $1,200? Well, the location to which you're flying is certainly a factor, but make no mistake! No matter where it is, it's expensive. There are ways to pay less for your tickets, but usually not *a lot* less. Even a discounted ticket is still going to cost several hundred dollars round-trip. What someone in your position needs is a way to fly to these places for just a little money...very little.

Probably the best deal in passenger flying to be found anywhere in the world is the opportunity to fly as an air courier. Although the full explanation of how the air courier setup works is quite long, I'll give you the abbreviated version.

Many businesses transport cargo from one country to another. But, when something is sent internationally, it must pass through customs. When cargo goes through customs, it can take days before it's released. This can be a real problem for time-sensitive material. However, if the shipment is sent as the personal baggage of a passenger, it goes through in minutes. The key, then, is to find a way to send the cargo as personal baggage.

Enter the air-courier opportunity. What businesses and courier services have found is that they can find international travelers who are willing to give up their excess baggage allowances in exchange for plane tickets that are dirt cheap. For example, let's say that you want to visit Rome, Italy, but can't afford the plane fare. No problem. By agreeing to give up your excess baggage allowance, you can receive your ticket for free (yes, that does happen) to Rome.

Now, you might be thinking at this point, *What good is traveling if I can't take any real baggage?* Well, that is a consideration. Flying this way may not be for everybody. However, if you're a hearty soul and can get by on whatever you can carry on to the plane, you'll be able to do it. (Don't underestimate how much you can pack into a carry-on bag, either. Many of these carry-on bags will hold a lot of clothing if you pack carefully.)

One of the real problems with flying as an air courier is that you can't take a family vacation this way. Children can't go as air couriers, and couriers must fly alone. So this is an opportunity for someone to take a trip by himself, usually. It should be stated, however, that it's possible for a couple to take a trip together if they work out the details. For example, a husband can leave as an air courier for a vacation destination one day, and his wife can join him in the same capacity later that day or the next. They can return in the same fashion, as well.

The air courier opportunity may not be conducive for long trips for most people (although it is possible to take a two-week trip as a courier). Rather, it's a good way for someone to take a quick jaunt out of the country for a few days to an exciting foreign location. Although you can book air courier flights on your own, I'd use a booking agent at first. For more information you can contact the Air Courier Association at 800-693-8333. There is a fee for their service. Also check out www.aircourier.org and www.courier.org. By the way, don't bother trying to book a flight unless you have a passport. The companies who use courier services are serious about getting their cargo delivered in a timely fashion. Therefore, the air courier companies will not risk letting them down by giving you a reservation on the basis that you're going to get a passport before the flight leaves. So make sure you have passport in hand before you call.

TAKING ACTION
Consider a free, working vacation.

You might be surprised to learn that you can actually enjoy a vacation for pretty close to free at some of the most beautiful, historical natural environs to be found anywhere. You don't believe me? Well, it's true, and what's more, there are a bunch of them out there to be had by anyone who's willing to cough up a little time and effort to help out at the very spot at which you'll be vacationing. Intrigued? Read on.

As you probably know, some of the most beautiful and desirable vacation spots in the country are state and federal parks. While the management and operation of these parks is handled principally by paid professionals, there are a lot of opportunities for volunteers. Volunteer help is so desirable at some of these locations that state and federal agencies are willing to let volunteers come and stay on site for free in exchange for their efforts in assisting park operations and research.

Perhaps the most common jobs for volunteers, for example, involve working as park hosts for visitors and as rangers of one kind or another. There are, however, more interesting jobs available, depending on where you want to go. You can help field researchers and scientists in many of the locations, and in other places you can work as a museum assistant and assistant archivist. Training for these jobs is free of charge, and, in general, you receive free housing and assistance with meals and other considerations.

Granted, these "vacations" may not be suitable for everyone, in part because they are not vacations in the purest sense of the word. You do have to spend some time working while you're at these sites. In some cases the work can be downright challenging. However, if you're up to it, you'll find that these are perhaps the best opportunities available for anyone with little money to vacation.

TAKING ACTION
Volunteer at a national or state park.

State and national park systems in the United States offer plenty of opportunities for volunteering that can be turned into low-cost, family vacations. Many volunteer positions in parks include free or nominal cost housing (camping sites/tent sites/cabins) and may also include equipment, uniforms, and even small stipends for expenses. Terms of service can range from one week to three months or more and vary in hours worked per day. How can you find out what's available and what you qualify for?

Check out the National Park Services (NPS) website at www.nps.gov. Go to the "Info Zone," click on "Volunteers," then click on "Opportunities." The listing of national parks includes volunteer needs. Follow the instructions for sending in applications. You can also contact the NPS coordinator for volunteers at 202-513-7141.

Most states have park services that also offer volunteer opportunities. These can range from "park hosts" to "trail guides." By using the internet (search: "state" "park" "volunteer"), you can find myriad opportunities to serve and experience nature firsthand! Another source of information is going to a specific state's website and looking under "state parks," "fish and wildlife," or "parks and recreation."

TAKING ACTION

Check out the Student Conservation Association.

The Student Conservation Association is designed to give adults the opportunity to work as volunteers in our national parks, wildlife refuges, forests, and other public lands. Participants must be at least 16 years of age, and be willing to work as assistants in areas including forestry, geology, trail maintenance, archaeology, and a host of other specialties designed to help preserve the environment and natural surroundings. The SCA program is free of charge, and provides accommodations (tents), all meals, and any equipment you'll need. Terms of service are usually

4 to 8 weeks long, but there are some opportunities for less time. You don't have to be a student to take advantage of this program! If you qualify, you can even receive financial aid.

TAKING ACTION
Stay at a hostel.

Staying at *hostels* is a low-cost alternative to staying at hotels. Contact Hostelling International/American Youth Hostels at 202-783-6161 (Washington, D.C.) or fax them at 301-495-6697. You can also find out where hostels are located, cost information, and other details at their website: www.hiusa.org. For reservations at a specific hostel, call 800-909-4776. Hostels are a cross between dormitories and military barracks, where guests share communal facilities, including a kitchen. Amenities and site services vary. There are 5,000 separate locations in 70 countries. The best part about hostels is the price. It's rare to find a hostel where you have to spend more than $20 per person per night.

Travel can be one of the most enjoyable experiences you will ever have. I can tell you that my times away with my family over the years have been some of the most treasured memories. Hand feeding a deer with my son in the Grand Canyon, going to France with my wife for a week, taking my daughter on a white water rafting trip, these are the memories that have been the most special. My hope is that this chapter will help you experience special times with your family. You *can* realize your travel dreams.

You Can Own
Your Home

For many of us, the representative benchmark of the American dream is home ownership. To have a physical piece of this country that you can call your own is a source of great pride to all who can lay claim to such ownership. Unfortunately, there are a lot of people who don't participate in this aspect of the American dream, because they can't afford to or they think they can't.

Rent revenues have climbed to such exorbitant levels in some markets these days that there is little month-to-month savings, if any, derived from renting a residence compared to purchasing one. The biggest obstacle to folks getting into homes of their own is usually the up-front money required to get their feet in the door (literally speaking).

This chapter is divided into two main sections. The first covers the subject of home purchasing. These money-saving topics include how you can buy a home of your own for as little up-front money as possible. The second section deals with the sale of a home, and offers sound advice for keeping the selling costs as cheap as possible so you keep more of your money.

Buying Your Home

TAKING ACTION

If you're short on cash, make the
FHA home your first priority.

If you desperately wish to have a home of your own but you don't have a lot of money to throw around, "down payment" can be one of the ugliest combination of words in the English language. If you try to buy a home with a conventional loan, you can expect to be asked to cough up 5% or more of the purchase price as a down payment. This means that even if you're in the market for a modest home that is selling for $100,000, you would have to put up around $5,000 or more—and that doesn't include the other associated costs of purchasing a home such as closing costs.

Fortunately, there is a government program out there with people like you in mind. The Federal Housing Administration (FHA) is an arm of the Department of Housing and Urban Development. One of its duties is to act as an insurer of home loans. The general idea behind this is that the government decided years ago that they wanted to make home ownership more accessible to more Americans. The FHA, then, serves to guarantee loans made by lenders who participate in its program. Because of this government guarantee, it is easier for prospective home buyers to qualify for the loans. As part of the program, the amount of down payment required is lower than it is with conventional loans. FHA loans require down payments of no greater than

5%—and in many cases the down payment can be as low as 3%. There are limits to how much of a home loan the FHA will insure. At last check, the limit was a little over $223,000.

To find out more about the home-buying opportunities available through the FHA, contact the Department of Housing and Urban Development field office nearest you. You may find it in the "Government Blue Pages" section of your telephone book. Also, any real estate agent in your area should be able to assist you.

If a down payment still seems too much to ask, there is now a wide variety of 100-percent loan programs available, even to people who have had credit problems such as a bankruptcy. These loans do require a higher interest rate. See www.parislending.com for assistance with these and other types of mortgage loans.

TAKING ACTION
Learn to work
with motivated sellers.

For a variety of reasons, the demand for homes is not what it once was. This doesn't mean that a home owner will be stuck for the rest of his life in his purchase, but it does mean that sellers who want to leave their current residences more quickly oftentimes must be willing to part with their homes under terms that are not as favorable to them as they would like. This is good news for you. A motivated seller will frequently do just about whatever it takes to sell his house. The key is for you to keep a sharp eye out for these opportunities and to have a clear understanding of unconventional sales mechanisms that appeal to desperate sellers.

In a nutshell, a motivated seller is one who is willing to part with his home in a fashion that requires the buyer to make no down payment or a very small one. (Sellers know that the lack of up-front money is what usually keeps buyers out of the market). There are a lot of ways that a seller who is truly motivated might be willing to work with you in this regard. Here are a couple of examples.

The "wrap-around" mortgage can be a very effective tool for you to use to get into a home. With the wrap-around mortgage, you give the seller a mortgage for the full price of the house, but at an interest rate that is roughly 2% higher than that which is on his current loan balance. Using this technique, the seller, while walking away from the table with no up-front money in his pocket, will receive a worthwhile amount of positive cash flow from the residence. What's more, if the seller has no loan balance of his own left on the house, this can be an even more attractive deal for him (or her), because the payment you send each month will not be offset by any payments he must make.

Another solid idea that might appeal to a motivated seller is the notion of receiving the down payment in the form of monthly payments. You could offer to pay the down in a predetermined number of monthly installments, along with the normal monthly payment due to him. You might even offer to pay interest on the unpaid portion of the down payment each month—if you think that might get the deal done.

Still another option is to propose to the seller that he accept a promissory note or equity interest in some other kind of property you own in lieu of a down payment. For example, if you own another piece of real property, you could write a note that's secured by the mortgage on the property you own, and use that as your down. If you own a car, boat, or something else that's similar in value and desirability, it would be easy for you to turn your interest in the property into a down payment by offering the property outright.

There are a lot of ways that a motivated seller might be willing to work with you so that he (or she) can get out of his house and move on with his life. The key is to be a motivated *buyer*, constantly looking for ways that you might be able to satisfy the seller's financial needs to at least a minimum level of acceptability. It is important that you not be shy about approaching motivated sellers with these kinds of suggestions. As long as you don't ask for a ridiculous degree of consideration from the seller, and you come across as sincere and thoughtful, you should never have a problem finding a seller who is willing to listen to what you have to say.

TAKING ACTION

If you're handy, consider buying a "fixer-upper."

When a house is on the market, a lot of emphasis is put into the cosmetics of the structure when determining a selling price. First impressions mean a lot. If a house is in need of obvious repairs like a fresh coat of paint, the replacement of porch trim, or the replacement of tile, sellers will be much too humble to ask for a price even close to what they would get if the house were in excellent condition. If enough of these kinds of repairs need to be done, the price of a home can be as much as 50% less than what it would be if the house were up to snuff. If you're at all handy with tools, this kind of house can represent one of the best deals you'll ever encounter in your lifetime.

While major repairs like electrical rewiring, substantial plumbing repairs, or framing concerns should always be handled by licensed and certified contractors, the little jobs are something most anyone with a little "handyman" skill can do without much difficulty. Even if you're not particularly adept at craftsmanship, you can at least slap on a respectable-looking coat of paint. In my experience, too few people give themselves enough credit when it comes to doing work like this. There are a number of guides published these days designed to instruct the inexperienced in a step-by-step fashion on doing minor home repairs. They are probably at your local library.

You can save a fortune if you look for a house like this. One warning: You should take care to make certain that the only types of repairs your target purchase needs are minor. If the house looks dilapidated enough, it may also be a signal that there are more substantial repairs that need to be done. If there are, they'll be uncovered when you have your home professionally inspected (which you *will* do) before you buy it. We'll talk more about this a little later.

TAKING ACTION
Be on the lookout for the lease-option.

The lease-option can be fairly categorized as a type of creative financing, but it has become so common as a sales mechanism for motivated sellers that it deserves a special section of its own.

In its barest form, the lease-option is the homeowner granting a renter the legal right to purchase the house he's currently renting at a particular point in the future for an agreed-upon price. An example of a lease-option agreement might be that a renter is given three years by the landlord (the homeowner) to purchase the home he's now renting for a price of $100,000. Typically, in a lease-option arrangement, the parties agree that a portion of the rent collected each month will be considered a partial payment toward the down payment in the event the renter chooses to exercise his option to buy. If the renter decides *not* to buy the property, he doesn't receive a refund of any kind. He is considered to have simply paid his rent obligation each month.

The lease-option arrangement is attractive to buyers who don't have much money to work with. Again, we have an option that does not demand the renter/buyer to come into the deal with any cash in hand beyond what's required to pay the first month's rent. These days, the lease-option has become very popular. A lot of sellers have found it a viable way to sell their home if they are willingly to part with the up-front money. If people who are selling their houses are amenable to the lease-option arrangement, they'll say so in their ads—just keep your eyes peeled.

TAKING ACTION
If the kitchen or bathroom needs renovating make it an issue.

Kitchens and bathrooms are two areas of a house that get the most attention from buyers. An old kitchen or bathroom—one that has fixtures, cabinets, tile, and so forth that are obviously outdated—significantly detracts from the interior decor of the home. As a result, a home that has problems in these areas should be selling for a fair bit of money below the fair market value of a home with more up-to-date personal areas.

If you look at a home that has a kitchen and/or bathroom that needs some renovating, even if it is in good condition but just doesn't seem up with the times, be certain to mention your concerns to the seller. People who know this business inside and out will tell you that an alert, aggressive buyer will be able to get, on average, another $5,000 off the asking price by making an issue of older bathrooms and kitchens.

TAKING ACTION

Look for a lender who is willing to waive the application fee.

There are a lot of costs you must bear when you buy a home, and many of them have to do with the mortgage. When you apply for a mortgage, you must pay an application fee. The purpose of the application fee is to process the application, although many people will tell you that there's nothing about the processing that's worth the several hundred dollars that the fee can cost you (application fees generally run anywhere from a couple of hundred dollars to as high as $500).

There is a lot of competition among lenders these days. The resulting "buyer's market" has allowed for more negotiation by prospective homeowners on areas of the sale that were once off-limits to such negotiation. The application fee is one such area. If you have a solid credit record and a steady income (you're an excellent mortgage candidate), you may be able to find a lender in your area who's willing to waive the application fee. Don't be shy about this. Your financial worthiness puts you in the driver's seat, so take advantage of it. If you can't find a lender who announces up front that he waives application fees as an incentive, *ask.*

TAKING ACTION
Make the lender pay for his own attorney.

One of the many costs associated with obtaining a mortgage from a lender is paying the lender's attorney to review the papers. Unfortunately, this cost is not usually borne by the lender, but by the purchaser.

Try not to pay this fee if you can help it. Again, the attorney who is reviewing these papers will be the lender's unless you have one of your own. You will *definitely* be expected to pay for his services. He will safeguard only the lender's concerns. I say, if the lender wants him, the lender should pay for him. My advice to you is to inform the lender up front that because his attorney is working exclusively for him, that he should pay the bill. If the lender fights you on this, consider moving on. If you are an attractive loan candidate, you should have no problem finding a lender who will agree to your demand (this is not an unreasonable request in the first place).

TAKING ACTION
Save money on your title insurance by getting a reissue rate.

If you don't have much money to work with, you need to try and save as much as possible at every turn in the home buying process. Take title insurance for example. Rather than purchasing a new title insurance policy, you can potentially save some money by getting a reissue rate. Assuming the seller has owner's title insurance, you should call his company to see if they offer a reissue rate. When a company offers a reissue rate, this means that they reissue the original policy to the new owner at a lower rate. Always ask.

TAKING ACTION
Home inspections—saving money by paying more.

You can decide to lower your moving costs (in the short run) by not having a qualified inspector check out your prospective purchase from top to bottom. However, given the fact that houses can be filled with potential problems and defects, you'd be taking an awful chance by doing that. Suppose the inspection would have uncovered problems with wood rot, bad wiring, or faulty plumbing? To fix any one of these problems (among a plethora of others an inspector might find) could cost you thousands. A proper home inspection will cost you no more than a couple of hundred dollars.

Once you've settled on a price for the home you want to buy, you will make a written offer to purchase. In this offer, make sure you state that you have the right to withdraw the offer if the results of the inspection are not satisfactory to you. Leave the wording of this contingency very general; give yourself every opportunity to back out of the deal if the inspector comes back with any negative information about the condition of the structure.

Selling Your Home

TAKING ACTION

Use several inexpensive home-improvement techniques to greatly enhance the value of your residence.

When you sell your home, common sense tells you that any creaky doors, broken switchplates, torn screens, or other obvious signs of disrepair should be fixed without fail. However, many people don't think about or choose to take those extra steps that, little as they may be, can greatly add to a home's attractiveness.

For example, for a relatively small sum of money you can invest in some flowers and plants and place them both inside and outside your home, as appropriate. The exterior of a home, when complemented by brightly colored flowers, looks noticeably and even strikingly appealing. If you don't believe me, look at an otherwise-decent home that has few, if any, flowers around it. There's a huge difference in appearance. As far as the interior of the home is concerned, the existence of some tall, distinguished plants in the halls or doorways, along with fresh flowers in the living room and on the dining room table, can go a long way toward making your house seem "homey."

Another tip is to place sweet-smelling aromatic oils on lamps in the house, to give your home added appeal. (Try to go for the smell that you believe best suits your home's decor and overall appearance.)

There are numerous ways to enhance the attractiveness of your house without costing you an arm and a leg. As a matter of fact, spending a lot of money to replace carpets or tile or such things in anticipation of putting your house on the market is ill-advised. The people who eventually buy your home may not share your tastes. They may decide to replace those things once they become the occupants. Keep things cheap and simple.

TAKING ACTION
Use brokers to help you decide the price at which your home should sell.

When you decide to sell your home, the most important factor you must consider is at what price to offer your residence. There are a number of ways to come up with a price—some better than others, some more expensive than others. Given your current circumstances, you certainly want to find the most accurate, most reasonable figure as cheaply as possible. There *is* a way to get a price from real-estate professionals for free.

The majority of real-estate companies offer "free, no obligation market analysis." Call several companies, make sure they offer this service, then invite several of them in to look at your property. Each agent will prepare a *competitive market analysis* (CMA) for you. The CMA will tell you how your house, in the respective opinion of each agent, compares to others in your neighborhood and at what price it should be offered.

You need to bear in mind, however, that each real-estate agent that gives you an analysis is hoping you will hire him (or her) to sell your house for you. Let them know that you haven't decided whether you should try to sell your house yourself or go through a real-estate broker. You can also mention that if you decide to try to sell your own home and it doesn't sell within a certain time period, you will be contacting a broker to help you.

TAKING ACTION
Use cost-effective services to help you settle on a price for your home.

You want to find the right price for your home, but you haven't got a lot of money to hire a quality appraiser. One suggestion, which I just outlined, involves contacting a bevy of brokers and garnering competitive market analyses. Another way is to contact a service that specializes in providing prospective sellers with relevant information about the sales of complementary houses in the same areas.

The internet is a great way to discover public information about real estate in your state. By going to a search engine and typing in "home price check" or entering www.inpho.com, you'll be able to enter a range of addresses to check the prices of houses that have recently been sold in your area.

TAKING ACTION
If you try to sell your house yourself, put a time limit on your sales efforts.

One of the best ways to save yourself a bundle of money in the sale of your home is to handle the transaction yourself. When *you* are able to successfully sell your home, you save thousands of dollars that would otherwise go to a broker as commission. This can be an especially easy proposition if you live in a desirable real property market because you may have to spend only a few weeks getting the deal done. For helpful information on selling your own home, go to www.christianmoney.com.

However, you must, as they say, know "when to say when." While successfully selling your own home can save you a bundle, it's not an easy task. You must deal with a lot of people who may not be making serious inquiries or who may not be qualified buyers. In these cases, you run the risk of this becoming one of those situations where trying to do something for less costs more in the long run.

A real estate agent or broker, simply by virtue of being in the business of selling properties, will be able to get the job done for you more quickly and more efficiently than you will be able to. That's a general fact. You may, however, have some good fortune and other circumstances relative to your personal situation that will enable you to sell the home within a matter of weeks or a few months. You should be prepared, however, to let the real-estate professionals take over after a certain period of time. I suggest giving yourself about three months to close the deal on your own. [This guideline varies depending upon your particular circumstances. For example, if you're in no rush whatsoever, you might give yourself longer, but beware. A house that has been on the market for quite a while tends to get a bad reputation on the part of potential buyers. It suggests that there may be something wrong with the property, or that the seller (you, in this case) may be difficult to work with.] In any event, remember that there are worse things than having to pay a real-estate commission. Plus, there are always ways to pay less than the standard industry commission that's charged. Read on and you'll see what they are.

If you opt to use a broker, consider a discounter.

A standard real-estate broker's commission is usually some-where in the neighborhood of 7%. This means that if you sell your home for $100,000, the broker will walk away with $7,000 of it. If you want to save as much of that money as possible, but would like the advantage of having at least some measure of pro-fessional real-estate assistance, consider the services offered by a discount broker or agent.

In general, there is not yet a bona fide category of real-estate brokers known as "discount brokers." If you were to look in the Yel-low Pages for a discounter, for example, you would have to look un-der the regular category of "Real Estate" and find one within that broad classification. (There may be some listings available under a classification "Real Estate—Discount Brokers.") Many of the real-estate companies that offer discount services say so in their ads, so be wide-eyed when perusing them. If you're not certain, call and ask.

Discount real-estate brokers' services come in all shapes and sizes. Some do little more than put the "For Sale" sign up in your yard, while others do just about everything a regular full-service broker does. The key is to shop around and track down the discount real-estate brokers and agents in your area. You may recognize some of the names of the better-known dis-count franchises like "Buy Owner" or "WHY USA" (WHY stands for "We Help You"), but there will be others in your area as well. Look for them.

If you do consider going the discount-broker route, make sure that any discounters you consider have the ability to list your home through the Multiple Listing Service (MLS) clearing-house in your area. This service ensures that your property will be seen by many brokers and potential buyers. This service is pretty much standard with any full-service broker, but not all discounters make it available. Be selective.

It is also possible to retain the services of a real-estate coun-selor, an expert in the area of real-estate transactions. This coun-selor will assist you in an ongoing fashion with the process, should you decide to handle most of the work yourself. Some counselors provide their services for 1% of the selling price of the home, while others will work with you on an hourly fee basis. If you would like to find out more about working with a counselor, con-tact The National Association of Realtors at 800-874-6500.

TAKING ACTION

Use a temporary listing contract to attract buyers who may be attached to agents.

If, in the course of trying to sell your home yourself, you come across a real-estate professional that knows of a potential buyer who will not do anything without an agent, it might be worth your while to strike up a special arrangement. I'm talking about doing business with an agent who believes he may have a "slam dunk" buyer for you. In this circumstance, consider the temporary listing contract.

The temporary listing contract is just what its name says. You sign a temporary listing agreement with the agent, wherein the terms of the deal with the agent are outlined. In general, the compensation to the agent is much lower than the standard 6% or 7% deal because you've done most of the work (it's usually going to be around 3%). The agreement will mention the prospective buyer by name, as well as the amount of time the agent has to bring you an offer from him (no more than a couple of days; if the interested parties are serious, this deal shouldn't take long).

The temporary listing contract is a good example of a "next best thing." Sure, it would be great if you could sell your home and pay no commission to anyone, but those deals don't always work out. By going through the temporary listing contract, you get the hands-on services of a real-estate professional for half or less of the normal cost.

TAKING ACTION
Try the "3% for agent's sale" route in your cost-cutting efforts.

One of the problems with trying to sell property on your own without going through an agent deals with the loyalties of the prospective buyers. If a buyer has been using an agent to find a suitable home, he may have a sense of loyalty toward the agent, who has probably done a lot of legwork on behalf of the buyer. Granted, the agent is not paid by the buyer but that's the point. A lot of buyers will feel funny about purchasing a "For Sale by Owner" property if there's no way for the agent who's been helping them out to get paid. Furthermore, if the agent has been charged by the buyer with handling the search for homes outright, then there's little chance (make that no chance) that your property will ever be seen by a represented buyer.

There's a way around this problem; however, it requires that you be willing to cough up some of the sales proceeds. If you make it known that an agent who sells your home will earn a reduced commission (such as 3%), then you won't have to deal with the fact that your home isn't receiving the audience exposure it could. For an agent to work with you like this, he will demand that you sign an open listing, an agreement that guarantees that you'll pay the stated commission if he brings you the eventual buyer. If you're willing to fork over 3% of the proceeds to an agent for bringing you the buyer, make certain that the advertisements and signs for the sale of your home indicate that fact.

TAKING ACTION
Always shop out the broker's commission.

While not everything in life is negotiable, a lot of things are. One thing that's definitely negotiable is a real-estate agent's commission. You'll find that the standard 6% to 7% "take" is something you can work around by shopping it out. Real-estate agents realize that the vast majority of the public believes real-estate commissions are carved in stone (and, thus, nonnegotiable). Not true. If anything in life *is* negotiable, it's commissions. Now, agents won't tell you that their rates are negotiable (for some, they aren't). So be it. The fact is, there are so many real-estate salespeople out there these days that if you look hard enough, you will find a regular, full-service broker who's willing to do the job for perhaps 4% or 5% instead of 6% or 7%. That could mean a savings of thousands for you...just for being willing to do a little legwork and shop more than a couple of brokers. Not bad!

Appendix

Affordable No-Load Mutual Funds

When choosing an investment, remember that the more research you do the better decision you will make. When it comes to mutual fund investing the most valuable research has to do with understanding your own risk tolerance—and finding a fund that matches your investment temperament. Clearly, knowing the fund's track record over a number of years, its manager, expense charges, and so on will make you an informed, smart investor. *Investors Business Daily* provides excellent resources for mutual fund investors. I also recommend *Kiplingers Personal Finance* magazine.

No-Load Mutual Funds
for $50 Per Month

The following fund companies, ("families"), will waive their initial lump-sum minimum investment requirements if you agree to enroll in their respective automatic investment programs. The families on this list ask that you agree to send at least $50 per month.

T. Rowe Price
800-638-5660
www.troweprice.com

American Century
800-345-2021
www.twentieth-century.com

Invesco
800-525-8085
www.invescofunds.com

Fremont Funds
800-548-4539
www.fremontfunds.com

Strong Funds
800-368-1030
www.estrong.com

Scudder Investments
800-728-3337
www.scudder.com

Dreyfus Founders Funds
800-525-2440
www.dreyfus.com

Best Web Sites for More
Information on Mutual Funds

Fund Index Yahoo
http://biz.yahoo.com/i

Mutual Fund Families—Yahoo
http://biz.yahoo.com/p/fam/a-b.html

Brill's Mutual Funds Interactive
http://www.fundsinteractive.com

Smartmoney—Funds
http://www.smartmoney.com/funds

Quicken—Mutual Fund info
http://www.quicken.com/investments/mutualfunds

Morningstar
http://www.morningstar.com

Yahoo's Mutual Fund Center
http://finance.yahoo.com/f0?u

Superstar Investor's Fund Links
http://www.superstarinvestor.com/fundlinks.html

Bibliography

Brobeck, Stephen and Kent Brunette. *Money in the Bank.* New York: Perigee Books, 1993.

Cortesi, Gerald R. *Mastering Real Estate Principles.* Chicago: Dearborn Financial Publishing, Inc., 1966.

Dowd, Merle E. *Money, Banking, and Credit Made Simple.* New York: Doubleday, 1994.

Editors of *Consumer Reports. The Consumer Reports Money Book.* Yonkers, NY: Consumer Reports Books, 1995.

Jones, John Oliver. *The U.S. Outdoor Atlas & Recreation Guide.* New York: Houghton Mifflin, 1994.

Kelley, Linda. *Two Incomes and Still Broke?* New York: Times Books, 1996.

Pivar, William H. *Power Real Estate Selling.* Chicago: Dearborn Financial Publishing, Inc., 1988.

Sloane, Leonard. *The New York Times Personal Finance Handbook.* New York: Times Books, 1995.

Other Good
Harvest House Reading

LIVING WELL ON ONE INCOME
by *Cynthia Yates*

Cynthia Yates shows you how to enjoy life more but spend less—on one income. Abundant personal stories, amusing anecdotes, and practical ideas invite you to a life of "one-income living with flair."

A HUSBAND AFTER GOD'S OWN HEART
by *Jim George*

Your marriage will grow richer and deeper as you pursue God and discover 12 areas in which you can make a real difference in your relationship with your wife.

A WIFE AFTER GOD'S OWN HEART
by *Elizabeth George*

One secret to marital bliss is for a wife to love her husband the way God designed for her to love him. The rewards for doing so are rich! Elizabeth George examines 12 insights to help you have a more fulfilling marriage.

WORKING AT HOME
by *Lindsey O'Connor*

Since the 1997 release of author Lindsey O'Connor's easy–to–use book *A Christian's Guide to Working from Home* the number of people choosing to launch home–based businesses has skyrocketed. In this updated version, *Working at Home*, Lindsey includes the latest information on this increasingly popular trend.

WHY MEN AND WOMEN ACT THE WAY THEY DO
by *Bill and Pam Farrel*

Building on the popularity of their "Waffles and Spaghetti" books, the Farrels combine humor with solid research in a book designed to help men and women move past conflicts caused by innate sexual differences.

HARVEST HOUSE
PUBLISHERS